BLACKWORK
EMBROIDERY
DESIGN AND TECHNIQUE

BLACKWORK EMBROIDERY
DESIGN AND TECHNIQUE

MARGARET PASCOE

B. T. BATSFORD LTD. LONDON

Frontispiece 'Elton John' by Maureen Haslam (1980).
Tutor, Hilary Cooper, Merton Adult Education Centre,
Surrey. 28×22 cm ($11 \times 8\frac{1}{2}$ in). Embroidered with
various black embroidery threads on grey linen, count
28/2.5 cm (1 in.).

© Margaret Pascoe 1986
First published 1986
First published in paperback 1989
Reprinted 1993

ISBN 0 7134 5146 7

Typeset by
Latimer Trend & Company Ltd, Plymouth
and printed in Great Britain by
The Bath Press
Avon

for the publishers
B. T. Batsford Ltd
4 Fitzhardinge Street
London W1H 0AH

Contents

Acknowledgments

Many years ago Moyra McNeill encouraged me to write a book on blackwork. I am sorry that she has had to wait so long and I welcome the chance to express my indebtedness to her, for much of my interest in the subject was stimulated by her sensitive teaching and writing.

Whilst writing this book I have been amazed and delighted by the good will extended to me from so many 'ordinary' embroiderers and professional bodies.

In collecting material I have had only one refusal and in all other instances the interest and help was unstinted. I have made many friends through this book and I trust that I have not lost any.

I would like to thank all who have so willingly lent their work to be photographed and made it easy for me to collect and return it; also the many friends who freely gave helpful criticism and advice. Their help and interest made me press on when I felt like giving up.

In all cases, unless otherwise stated, the photography is by my husband, Jim Pascoe. I am more than grateful to him for all the time and energy he spent in making a 'proper job' of this exacting task; without his help this book would have been poorer in so many respects.

MP
West Molesey, 1986

Introduction

Stephan Hirzel, in his foreword to *Creative Drawing: Point and Line*, says: 'This book is in no way meant to incite dull imitation but should rather act as a starting point for further original development.' I cannot think of a better way of stating what I wish to achieve.

When learning a practical technique such as embroidery there is no real substitute for attendance at a class led by an experienced teacher. Here the student will see demonstrations and handle samples of unfinished and finished work. There will be the invaluable give-and-take between students as well as the advice of the teacher. It is surely the best way of learning.

Unfortunately, not all would-be embroiderers have access to such classes and a practical do-it-yourself book is the next best thing. In the following pages I have tried to help such students.

I start with a chapter on the development of blackwork from the earliest authentic records at the beginning of the sixteenth century, up to the present day. In the chapters which follow I have tried to help the student by giving practical suggestions on inspiration, design, materials, methods of sewing and presentation.

Throughout the book there are illustrations of modern pieces with comments. These pieces were chosen to show the great variety possible within the bounds of the technique. The photographs of embroidery have been made with the grain of the fabric shown prominently where possible, to help you copy the patterns if you wish.

I find that copying is easier to do directly upon a piece of evenweave material, rather than by first making a stitch diagram on squared paper. In the same way, I find it easier to create new patterns directly upon a piece of fabric. This is a personal

1   A motif inspired by a drawing of a fir cone, embroidered by Mary Chandler, 1984, at the London College of Fashion; tutor, Anthea Godfrey. 10 cm (4 in.) square. Embroidered with five graded thicknesses of black silk on natural linen, count 28/2.5 cm (1 in.).

preference, and many embroiderers like to work from stitch diagrams. Throughout the book I include both photographs of stitches and stitch diagrams, the latter particularly for the more complicated patterns. I hope that you will feel sufficiently independent to adapt them or to invent your own patterns, as embroiderers have done through the centuries.

During my research in the library of The Embroiderers' Guild into the origins of blackwork I was delighted to find this passage in an article by May Morris:

Another notable type of line embroidery is seen in the beautiful and delicate Holbeinesque and Elizabethan blackwork on white linen or silk. The outlines – a flower garden, save for colour – are strongly and broadly marked, and the filling of flower and fruit and stem and butterfly is done in horizontal lines of stitches infinitely fine – little diaper patterns, delicate and ingenious and patient beyond telling: only a spider's web is more lightly woven.

To me Mary Chandler's motif (fig. 1) is a delightful example of blackwork which is both delicate and ingenious.

1. The development of blackwork

Blackwork is a counted-thread technique which is built up from the simplest of all embroidery stitches – a short straight stitch made over two or more threads of an evenweave fabric. A combination of many such stitches can make lines or geometrical patterns which may be isolated or connected. The term Holbein stitch or, more technically, double running stitch, is used when the simple stitches make a continuous line. Double running stitch was a form of decoration on costume at the beginning of the sixteenth century.

Evidence for the early use of blackwork comes from portraits and religious paintings, particularly from the works of Hans Holbein the Elder (*c.*1465–1524) and his son Hans Holbein the Younger (1497–1543). The earliest definite example of blackwork I can find is from a religious work by Hans Holbein the Elder painted in 1516 (fig. 2). The representation of the stitching is so clear that I was able to produce stitch diagrams (fig. 3) and a sampler (fig. 4).

I know of no firm evidence for the existence of blackwork before 1516. Stone and brass memorials are a form of portraiture and a guide to the costumes of the period, but it is impossible to distinguish between blackwork and lace on them.

In the early examples of blackwork from this period there were no diagonal (slanting) stitches. The embroidery thread rigidly followed the direction of either the warp or the weft so that when a line changed direction, it did so through a right angle. This gives early blackwork a characteristically craggy effect.

In 1526, Hans Holbein the Younger painted the 'Burgomaster Meyer's Madonna' which is now in the Schlossmuseum, Darmstadt, West Germany. Anna Meyer is shown in her bridal gown with other

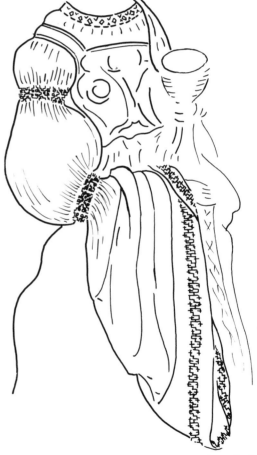

2 Sketch of part of the gown of St Barbara from the St Sebastian altar, painted by Hans Holbein the Elder, 1516, showing three blackwork bands on the sleeve. The pattern around the neckline is too indistinct to identify as blackwork. The work is now in the Alte Pinakothek, Munich, Germany.

9

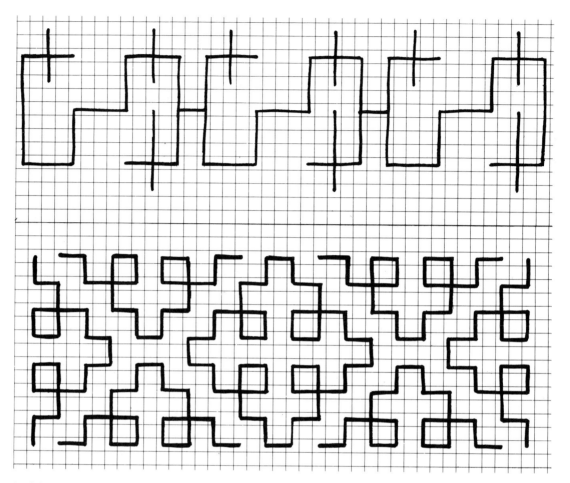

3 Stitch diagram for the two blackwork patterns in fig. 2.

members of the Meyer family. In addition to goldwork, the gown is embroidered with four blackwork patterns (fig. 5). The craggy, castellated appearance is very obvious in these patterns.

As far as we can gather from documents, portraits and surviving pieces, blackwork was embroidered on garments, bed linen and other household articles. The collars and cuffs of shirts and blouses worn under thicker outer clothes were embroidered with black stitches. At first, this stitching appears as a narrow black edging to a simple gathered frill, or as a seam decoration. It gradually becomes more complex and covers larger areas. During the second half of the sixteenth century, sleeves and sometimes whole bodices were completely covered with intricate patterns. The patterns were generally con-

tained within the bold outlines of leaves, petals and branches composed into a flowing design.

The repeating patterns were made using short running stitches worked over the threads of the linen. They are known as diaper patterns. These are also to be found as filling and border patterns in illuminated manuscripts in the Middle Ages. I have found that the word 'diaper' is not always understood. It is a term associated with weaving patterns, which are necessarily formed from short straight lines. A white fabric called diaper was made which had a raised woven pattern on the surface. It was absorbent and similar to our huckaback towelling, and before Terry towelling and the modern disposables was used as a baby's nappy; hence the American term 'diaper'.

An infinite variety of patterns can be made by combining horizontal, vertical and diagonal lines of varying lengths, with the thread always passing between the threads of the material, never through

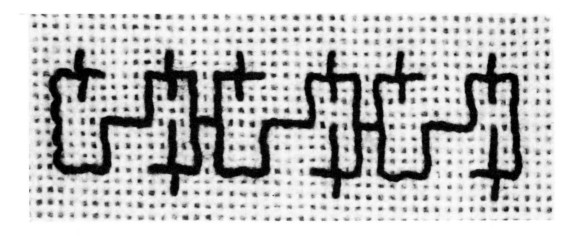

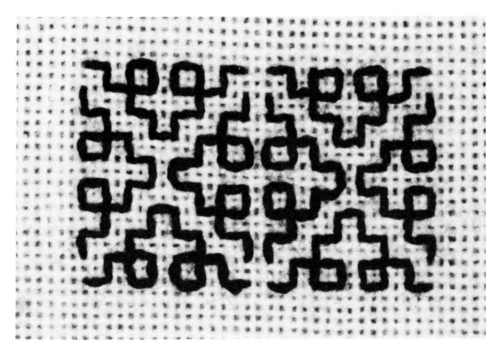

4 Samplers embroidered from diagrams of fig. 3. Black buttonhole silk on a furnishing hopsack, count 24/2.5 cm (1 in.).

them. Further variation can be obtained by altering the length of the spaces between the stitches and the thickness of the embroidery thread.

Caps and other head-dresses as well as pillow cases and bed covers were also decorated, and small amounts of gold thread were sometimes added to the blackwork. These articles were made of linen or cambric and would have been washed regularly with the harsh alkaline soaps of those days. It is not surprising that very few have survived for us to handle. The black dye used for the thread (known as Spanish silk) contained iron which made it more liable to rot, and in some cases produced iron-mould in the linen.

In contrast to these everyday articles the gold-embroidered ecclesiastical and secular ceremonial embroideries have survived. This is probably because of the care given to them by religious houses and professional establishments, as well as

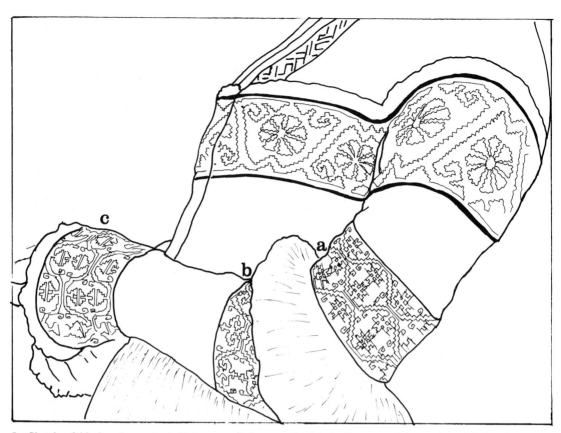

5 Sketch of blackwork on the bridal gown of Anna Meyer.

6 Stitch diagrams of three of the blackwork patterns from the sleeve of Anna Meyer's gown.

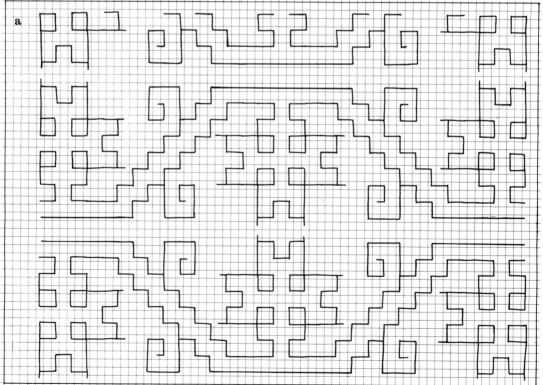

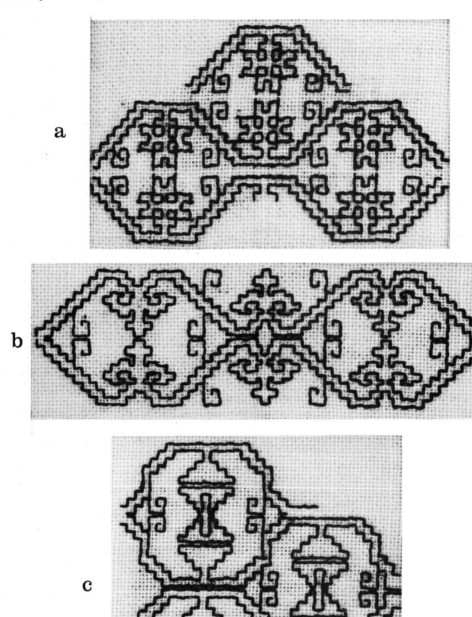

7 Samplers from diagrams of fig. 6 embroidered on furnishing hopsack, count 24/2.5 cm, (1 in.), using black buttonhole silk.

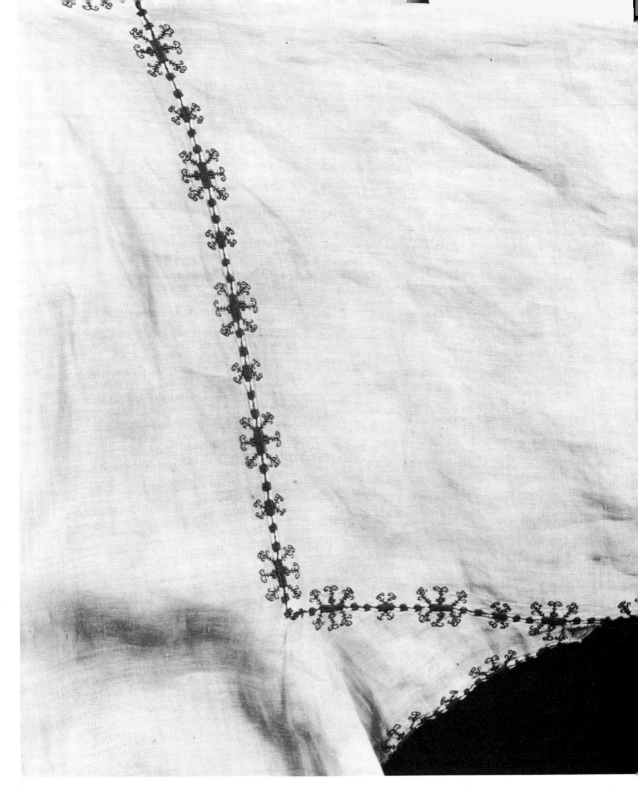

8 Seam decoration on a young man's shirt, *c.* 1545.
*(Photograph (reference number 112–1972) by permission of
the Victoria and Albert Museum, London.)*

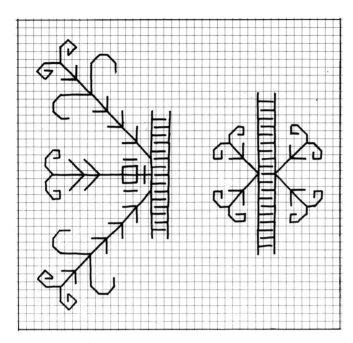

9 Stitch diagram derived from fig. 8.

10 Sampler embroidered from the diagram in fig. 9. Black buttonhole silk on natural linen, count 20/2.5 cm (1 in.). In the original, knotted buttonhole stitch holds the pieces of the shirt together.

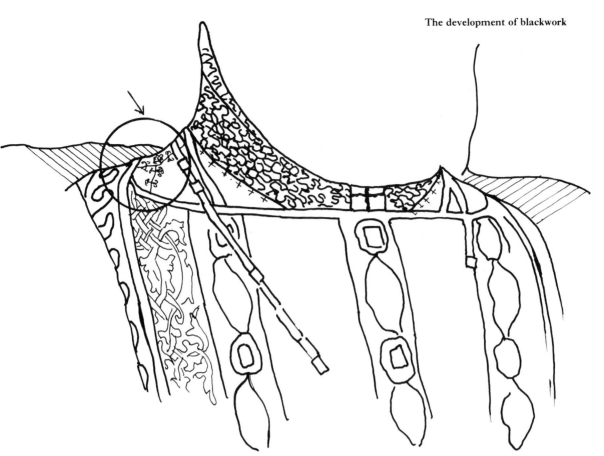

the more durable nature of the threads used. There are pieces of blackwork in museums which have gold threads still intact, but the pattern of the black stitching is indicated only by the holes made by the passing of the now rotted threads.

The embroiderers of the Tudor period copied their designs from pattern books. These became available in the sixteenth century following the invention of printing in Germany, and were used as a source of design in many crafts. One of the patterns on the sleeve of St Barbara (fig. 2) appears in a German pattern book of the same period. Only a few of these books survive, as the patterns were pricked through the printed page to transfer the design on to the fabric using the 'prick and pounce' technique.

In the late sixteenth and early seventeenth centuries the leaves and petals, which earlier had been filled with diaper patterns, were shaded with speckling stitches. In this way they imitated the illustrations in contemporary books printed from wood blocks.

So far I have referred only to geometrical patterns either worked in linear form or separated into

11 Sketch of seam decoration from a portrait of Henry VIII by Hans Holbein, *c.* 1536. Lugano-Castagnola, Thyssen-Bornemisza Collection. The seam (ringed in diagram) on the shirt, below an ornate collar heavily embroidered in gold, has the same blackwork motif as in fig. 8.

diaper patterns. Many of the black and white designs popular in Tudor times appear to be embroidered in satin stitch, chain stitch, stem stitch and so on, and for the purpose of this book are not considered to be true blackwork.

In the fifteenth and early sixteenth centuries there is documentary evidence of the existence of black embroidery in inventories of the possessions of wealthy citizens and in bequests; sometimes it is called Spanish work. From such meagre descriptions it is not possible to be certain that it is blackwork which is meant. Many authors connect the term Spanish work with Catherine of Aragon, the first wife of Henry VIII and daughter of Isabella and Ferdinand, joint rulers of Spain. One of her emblems was the pomegranate and in the

12 Detail from a long pillow cover, black silk on linen. Note the large vine leaves outlined in chain stitch and filled with diaper patterns. (*Photograph (reference number T.79.1924) by permission of the Victoria and Albert Museum, London.*)

13 Stitch diagram of the diaper pattern from fig. 12.

14 Sampler from the diagram in fig. 13. Black buttonhole silk on white linen, count 28/2.5 cm (1 in.).

15 Late sixteenth–century spray motif from the collection of the late John Jacoby, now in the possession of the Embroiderers' Guild. 12.5 cm (5 in.). Embroidered in black silk on very finely woven linen. Outlined in gold chain stitch.

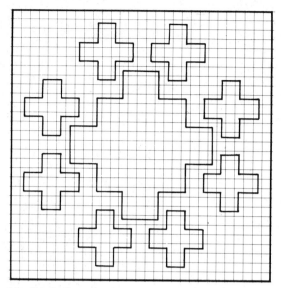

16 Stitch diagram of one diaper pattern from fig. 15.

17 Modern sampler of patterns from fig. 15, embroidered in black buttonhole silk on white linen, count 28/2.5 cm (1 in.).

simplified form of a diaper pattern this is still used today. Examples will be found throughout this book. Examples of Catherine's ecclesiastical work are preserved at Stonyhurst College in Lancashire, but there is no blackwork among them. Again, this could be because of its lack of durability.

The term blackwork can be applied to coloured embroidery. The majority of historical samples have black stitching but a few show red, green or blue stitching. On the whole, it was a monochrome technique relieved occasionally with gold. Blackwork refers more to the type of stitching and the patterns used than to the colour of the threads.

A few examples of blackwork are found in early Stuart times but little is heard of it again until the twentieth century; however, Mrs Archibald Christie does illustrate a sampler from Spain dated 1772 in her *Samplers and Stitches* (1929).

May Morris, daughter of the artist William Morris, refers in an article (1902) only to sixteenth-century blackwork and does not mention any later examples. *Weldon's Guide to Fancy Work* (1904) includes many forms of embroidery, but not blackwork.

One colleague of mine has suggested that this gap in the history of blackwork applies equally to most

18 Portrait of Capt Thomas Lee, 1594, by Marcus Gheeraerdts, 1561–1635. Captain Thomas Lee was a nephew of Sir Henry Lee, Queen Elizabeth's Champion of the Tilt. He is wearing what is probably a masque costume, with a long shirt draped up around his thighs. Janet Arnold, in an article entitled 'Elizabethan and Jacobean Smocks and Shirts' (1977), says that it is derived from a plate in a book printed in Antwerp in 1581. The diaper patterns filling the leaves and petals are simple. (*Photograph (reference number T.3028) by permission of the Tate Gallery, London.*)

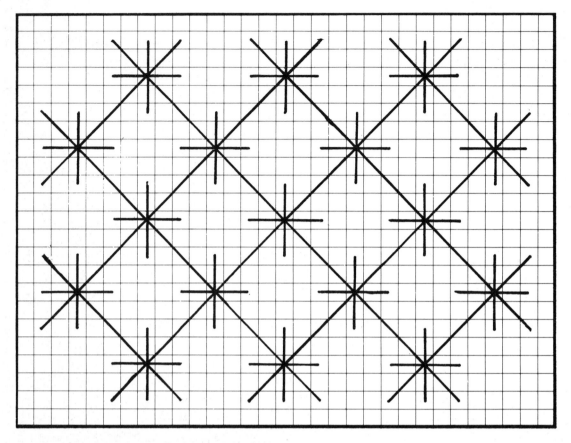

19   Stitch diagram derived from fig. 18.

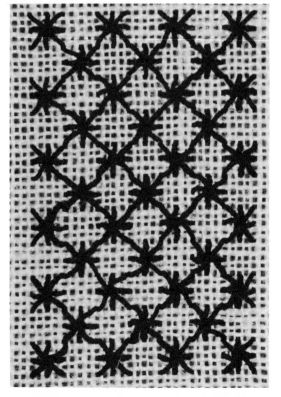

counted-thread work, apart from canvas work which was popular with the Victorians.

When blackwork first reappears in the twentieth century it is generally restricted to household articles such as cushion covers, tablecloths, tray cloths and so on. The stitch patterns of the early twentieth century were the same as those used in the sixteenth century, and great care was taken to make the work reversible, that is, the pattern was the same on the back as on the front and no loose ends of embroidery threads were visible (see fig. 21). In many pieces a strong outline was embroidered around the shapes filled with the patterns, and for cloths a hem was made in which the ends could be hidden. The outlining stitch was often chain or stem stitch, or a couched thicker thread. In the literature of the time a strong outline was regarded as an artistic neces-

20   Modern sampler of the diaper pattern in fig. 19. Black buttonhole thread on linen, count 28/2.5 cm (1 in.).

21   Tray cloth embroidered by the late Olive Prior in Stockbridge, Hampshire, 1930. 42 × 30 cm (16½ × 12 in.). The embroidery thread was Star Sylko (similar to a fine perlé) on natural linen, count 30/2.5 cm (1 in.). The narrow hem is finished with four-sided stitch. The pomegranate stitch around the border gives a link with Catherine of Aragon, whose symbol it was.

sity. Mrs Christie says in *Samplers and Stitches*: 'a firm decided outline is a necessary finish to these fillings' and in *The Sampler Book of Decorative Needlework* by L. Judd Morris (Dryad Press) emphasis is laid on 'an outline to hold the lighter parts together'.

Osyth Wood (Mrs Thomas Wood) was a notable embroideress in the period between 1925 and 1960. She lived in East Anglia, and embroidered exquisitely using many techniques. The Embroiderers' Guild has several pieces of blackwork embroidered by her; these, like all her work, are of an exceptionally high standard, and should be seen by students of the subject. I can only show two examples here,

but there is in *Embroidery*, 23 (1972), p. 117, an illustrated article about her entitled 'A Mid Twentieth Century Needlewoman'.

The traditional rules which determined what one could and could not do in embroidery continued to dominate until about 1960. After this, embroidery became more innovative and the restrictions imposed by tradition progressively lost their influence. This freedom meant that in blackwork more panels and hangings were embroidered and its use for household articles and clothing decreased.

The small stitch patterns seen from Tudor times are today used to create varied tonal areas; outlining is used only when needed for emphasis, and many different thicknesses of thread are used in one piece of work. Within each tonal area the pattern used is not uniformly stitched, but varied by adding or subtracting lines, and made thicker and thinner by using different threads.

Thus an effect is produced which is more like an etching than an overall uniform pattern. In this

23

22(a) Edge of a runner embroidered by Osyth Wood in 1929, showing 15 crinoline ladies named alphabetically from Amelia to Osyth Wood, each with a different blackwork pattern on her dress. Crinoline ladies wearing poke bonnets were a popular subject for embroidery in the 1920s and 1930s. I had always imagined that a part of their popularity was due to the fact that if the lady was wearing a poke bonnet in profile, no face needed to be embroidered. Osyth Wood was obviously not afraid of faces, and all her ladies face us frankly. 125 × 47.5 cm (50 × 19 in.), on fine natural linen.

22(b) Detail from fig. 22(a). The last of the ladies in the line.

23   A tray cloth in which each leaf and petal is outlined with stem stitch and filled with diaper patterns. The date of the work is uncertain but it is definitely in the style of the 1930s. Fabric, fine linen; 60 × 40 cm (24 × 16 in.)

24   Stitch diagrams of two of the patterns used by Osyth Wood.

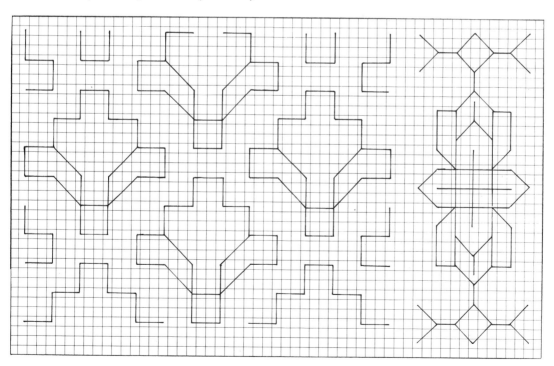

25 Sampler of stitches and patterns derived from them, inspired by Osyth Wood's work.

26 Cushion cover embroidered by Mary Thomson, Surrey, from a transfer published in a woman's magazine of the early 1950s. With the transfer were directions for obtaining the fabric and threads, and the stitches to be used. The fabric is a thick beige cotton crash, count 20/2.5 cm (1 in.), and the thread a no. 5 perlé. The cherries are embroidered with chain stitch in red perlé. The outlines are in stem stitch.

27

27 'Mushrooms' by Vanessa Stansfield. This small panel, 13 × 15 cm (5 × 6 in.), embroidered in 1984 at the Beckenham Adult Education Centre, illustrates the break away from heavy outlining. The design is divided into tonal areas produced by varying the thickness of the thread and the density of the diaper patterns. Embroidered with brown threads on cream Hardanger fabric, count 22/2.5 cm (1 in.). Mounted with a window mount covered in unbleached calico.

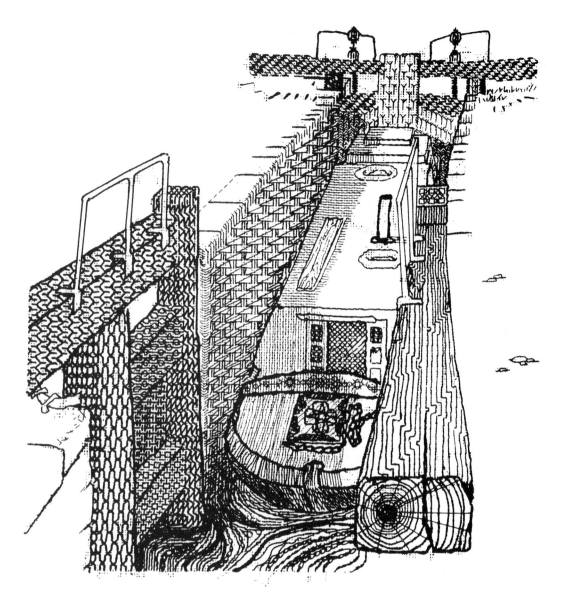

NARROW BOAT IN LOCK

28 'Narrow Boat in Lock', by Patricia Gaffer, Leicester, 1982; tutor, Wendy Williams. The design is reminiscent of an etching or woodcut. Blackwork patterns are used freely; long threads taken over as much as 1.3 cm ($\frac{1}{2}$ in.) of fabric are used to give the appearance of the grain of wood and the swirl of water. The pomegranates on the lock mechanism once again show the connection with the sixteenth century. 20 cm (8 in.) square, natural linen, count 20/2.5 cm (1 in.), embroidered with varying thicknesses of black thread. The work was based on a drawing by Maurice Poole.

way, to my mind, modern work is dramatic and dynamic and can express many moods.

Olive West, a piece of whose work is shown in fig. 120, wrote the following when I asked some students to write down what they felt about blackwork. She grew up in an era when embroidery was traditionally controlled. I found her remarks about modern work apt, and I think they express what many embroiderers feel about embroidery trends in general.

I have always been interested in traditional blackwork, mainly because of the great variety of patterns which can be made by the use of simple stitches in one colour.

Although the original blackwork was very controlled it seemed to me to have a subtler approach than most forms of canvas work. When I realized that blackwork could be employed in a freer, modern concept I enjoyed adapting this technique. I found that the creation of new stitches and combinations of stitches followed easily.

29 'Starlight Express' (detail) by Jillian White, 1984, Woking Adult Education Centre; tutor, Pamela Watts. An example of mixed techniques embroidered in blue-green threads on a fine, countable calico. The background was masked and sprayed with coloured inks. Blackwork stitches are used over the sprayed area. The hair plaits are made prominent using rows of Portuguese knot stitch. The exaggerated ear ornament is made of freely hanging chenille threads with glass beads. Also used are spangles, silver lurex thread and applied silver fabric.

Mixing different techniques can be helpful in getting the required effect; for example, appliqué and spraying with paint or dyes can give variety and emphasis. Some of these are dealt with in Chapter 9.

I am greatly indebted to numerous authors for their books on the history of blackwork, which stimulated me to undertake my research. I am not a professional historian, but I am fascinated by history;

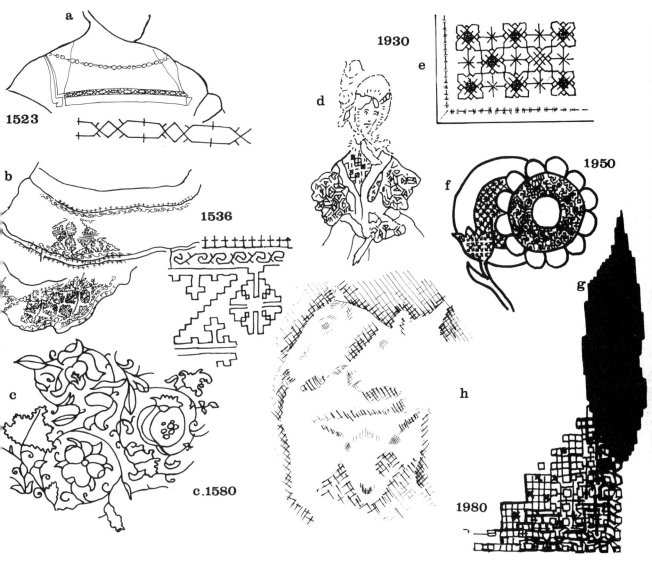

30 Sketch to illustrate the development of blackwork:
(a) A narrow band embroidered across the neckline from a portrait of Madame de Canaples, by Jean Clouet, 1523, in the National Gallery of Scotland, Edinburgh. An enlargement of the embroidery is also drawn.
(b) An embroidered cuff from a portrait of Jane Seymour by Hans Holbein, 1536, in the Kunst Historisches Museum, Vienna, Austria. See also the stitch diagram in fig. 134. The painting shows the complete reversibility of the embroidery.
(c) The outlines of a late sixteenth-century design on a sleeve in the National Museum of Antiquities of Scotland, Edinburgh. The flowing, curved plant stems, with flower and leaf shapes, are all filled with diaper patterns; gold threads have been added.

(d) 1930s. A crinoline lady with blackwork patterns on her clothing; all areas distinctly outlined.
(e) 1930s. A corner of a tray cloth with traditional diaper pattern.
(f) 1950s. Plant forms filled with diaper patterns, heavily outlined.
(g) 1980. Modern blackwork, with strong contrast of black and white. Randomized square diaper pattern at base. Work by a Manchester Polytechnic degree student, by kind permission of Anne Butler Morrell.
(h) 1984. 'Sheep', see fig. 36. Fabric sprayed with ink, and embroidered with free diaper patterns.

my main intention is to tell of the origins and evolution of an embroidery form which I find exciting. This is a very abbreviated and personal view. Why not tackle some of the books and articles listed at the end of the book, and judge for yourself?

Most of the portraits and embroideries I have referred to are on public view. Also, you can spend many enjoyable hours 'spotting the blackwork' when you visit museums and stately homes. In this leisurely pastime I have found bifocal spectacles a disadvantage and a magnifying lens a necessity.

Let me give one word of warning. In Tudor times aspiring gentry hired minor artists to copy portraits painted by famous painters, and hung the copies in their long galleries. They seem to have been a Tudor status symbol. The paintings were often inferior and inaccurate. The practice has continued down the ages even to the present time, and I urge you to make a few discreet enquiries before thinking that you have discovered a hitherto unknown sixteenth-century blackwork painting. You should be so lucky! But then again, who knows?

A short reading list for those interested in the history of blackwork is given at the end of this book. For serious students of the topic, I recommend a visit to the library of the Victoria and Albert Museum in London.

2. Inspiration for pattern and design

Glory be to God for dappled things –
    For skies of couple-colour as a brinded cow;
    For rose-moles all in stipple upon trout that swim;
Fresh-firecoal chestnut-falls; finches' wings;
    Landscape plotted and pieced – fold, fallow, and
    plough;
    And all trades, their gear and tackle and trim.

All things counter, original, spare, strange;
    Whatever is fickle, freckled (who knows how?)
    With swift, slow; sweet, sour; adazzle, dim;
He fathers-forth whose beauty is past change:
        Praise him.

                Gerard Manley Hopkins, 'Pied Beauty'

As I look around me I am conscious of many delightful patterns. In this chapter I can mention only a few that suggest blackwork embroidery to me, and hope to inspire you to find your own. Acute awareness of the world around us is a very great bonus which comes with the study of art.

Constance Howard, in *Inspiration for Embroidery*, has helped many to become aware of patterns and design in everyday life, and such television series as David Attenborough's *Life on Earth* and the accompanying books have beautiful photographs of natural patterns.

Pattern has an element of repetition, though not necessarily exact, accurate repetition. Whereas one spot on a deer would be seen as a blemish, dappling is a thing of beauty. There are markings on plants: variegated leaves, leaf mosaics, lines on barks, lichens, spots and gills on fungi, and annual rings on felled trees. Among the other natural phenomena which surround us are frost patterns and raindrops on glass, and on a larger scale in land-scapes, the patchwork effect of 'fold, fallow, and plough'. On the seashore there are wave patterns, markings in the sand, strata in the cliffs, shells, stones, barnacles and fossils.

Leaves, branches, trees and shrubs as well as animals and humans all have individual shapes. Grouped together these make other shapes in between and sometimes overlap to produce inter-esting patterns. Animal markings range from those on tabby cats to tigers, zebras and giraffes. Birds, their feathers and the shapes made by parts of their bodies such as wings, breasts, caps, crests and tails can be interpreted in embroidery.

Photographs of microscopic sections of living tissues are a wonderful source of inspiration. Browse through the pages of biology textbooks in your local library until something catches your eye. On looking at these patterns you will notice that very few are equally dense over the whole area, and individual units of the pattern vary in size. This is part of the attraction, in the same way that a house built of hand-made bricks is more attractive than one made of exactly uniform elements. Remember this when filling shapes, especially large ones, with patterns.

When it comes to man-made objects, the rela-tionship to blackwork pattern is perhaps more obvious. From earliest times, Man, surrounded by a wealth of natural pattern, has added more of his own. Some patterns were practical, others were of religious significance, and some were made simply for the joy of self-expression. Perhaps the most exuberant of these patterns is the Moresque deco-ration seen in mosques, and in the Alhambra in Granada, the residence of the Spanish monarchs after the defeat of the Moors in 1492. The abstract geometrical designs in this elaborate decoration are

31 'Field at Compton 1979', by Elizabeth Heitzman, Berkshire, tutor Valerie Campbell-Harding. 28 × 21 cm (11 × 8 in.). White Moygashel dress fabric, count 30/2.5 cm (1 in.), masked and sprayed with diluted black ink. Free blackwork stitches worked over the sprayed areas. Various black threads are used; there is some silver thread used discreetly in the sky and white perlé on the roofs of cottages. See article by Valerie Harding, 'Blackwork and Spraying', *Embroidery*, 30 (1979), p. 112.

32 Close-up of teazle, a natural pattern.

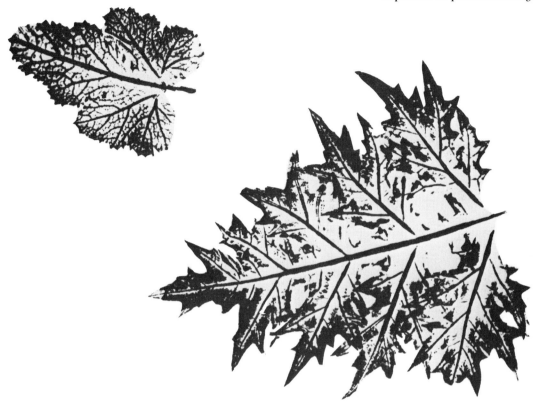

33 Ink prints of leaves.

34 Leaf motif from a small tablecloth by Diane Black-more, 1983, Buckinghamshire. Pale yellow cotton even-weave fabric, count 30/2.5 cm (1 in.), embroidered with two thicknesses of brown perlé thread. The diaper pattern is the same as that used in fig. 1.

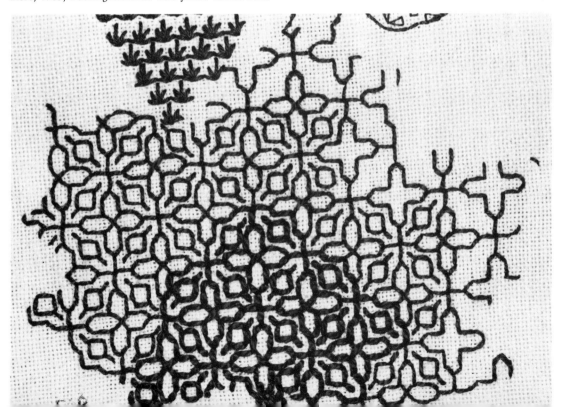

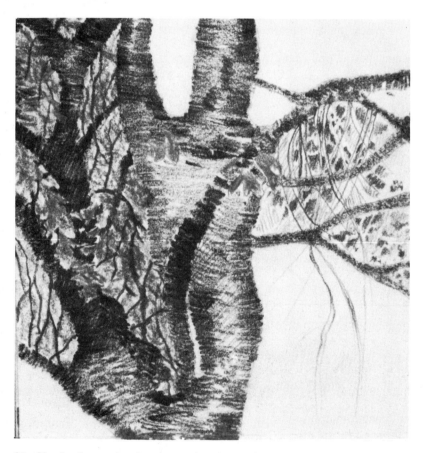

35 Sketch of a tree in a London garden. Some of the shapes between branches are filled with pattern. If you look at wood engravings, particularly through a magnifying lens, you will get ideas for blackwork to fill these shapes.

36 'Sheep', by Jenny Chippindale, 1984, London College of Fashion; tutor, Anthea Godfrey. 20 cm (8 in.) square. Coarse linen, count 22/2.5 cm (1 in.), sprayed before embroidering. Threads of varying thicknesses are used in white and shades of brown. This is a very pleasing group of sheep, creating more shapes between the bodies.

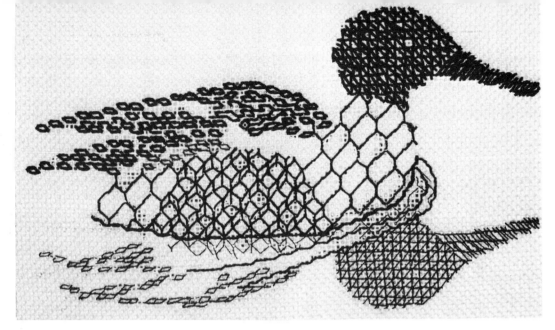

37 'Shoveller', by Pat Roberts, 1984, Woking Adult Education Centre; tutor, Pamela Watts. 16 × 10 cm (6 × 4 in.). Embroidered in various thicknesses of black thread on white linen, count 20/2.5 cm (1 in.). The reflection is embroidered using the same stitches as in the body of the duck, but with finer threads. The inspiration came from a magazine illustration.

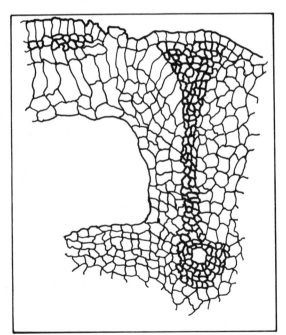

38 Drawing of section of a leaf under the microscope.

39 'Cat', by Vanessa Stansfield, 1984, Beckenham Adult Education Centre. 29 × 19 cm (11½ × 7½ in.). Embroidered in black threads of varying thicknesses on white linen, count 26/2.5 cm (1 in.). The white areas of the cat are left unembroidered; our eyes fill in the outline.

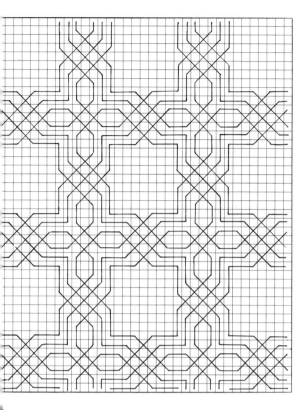

close to the Tudor blackwork patterns. The interchange of people and materials between the courts of Europe in the sixteenth century led to Moresque patterns from Spain being introduced into many countries, including Tudor England. The use of the pomegranate (an emblem of the Spanish court) in blackwork patterns has already been mentioned.

Cast- or wrought-iron balconies, gates and grilles are both decorative and functional. When looking at their transparent and delicate appearance, blackwork immediately springs to mind. Walls made of brick, stone or patterned blocks, fences, gates, ventilators, chimneys, roofs, slates, floor and wall tiles, pavings, flints, cobbles and many other building materials can be sources of inspiration. Highrise blocks with their window patterns, boats at moorings and cars in car-parks all show repetitive shapes. Ceramic pots and pipes of all shapes and sizes have patterned markings on them, and their shapes make patterns when grouped together.

Lettering creates many patterns, which were used frequently in Arabic art. It is not easy to adapt the modern European alphabet to blackwork patterns, but in the next chapter, we shall see that it has its uses when considering tone values.

40(a)   Stitch diagram constructed from wall decoration at the Alhambra, Granada, Spain.   **b**
(b) Sampler from diagram in fig. 40(a). Black, medium thickness, no. 45/3 silk on a slubbed off-white furnishing fabric, count 24/2.5 cm (1 in.).

41 Four motifs inspired by wrought-iron work, by Margaret Pascoe: each 13 × 10 cm (5 × 4 in.). These were embroidered at various times in the 1970s. Different thicknesses of black and red threads were used, with a small amount of gold thread.

42 Early eighteenth-century wrought-iron window screen from Steyr, Austria.

43 Sketch of a dry-stone wall, Derbyshire. Note that the variations in the sizes and shapes of the stones add interest.

44 Drawings from modern houses: brickwork and tiles suggesting blackwork patterns.

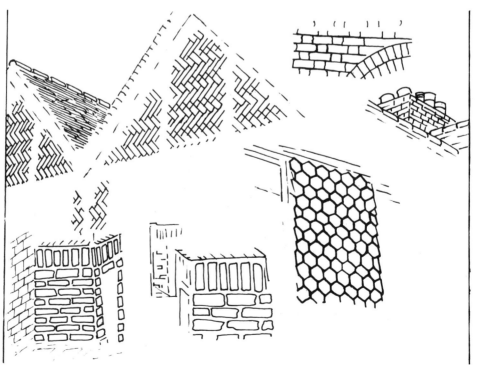

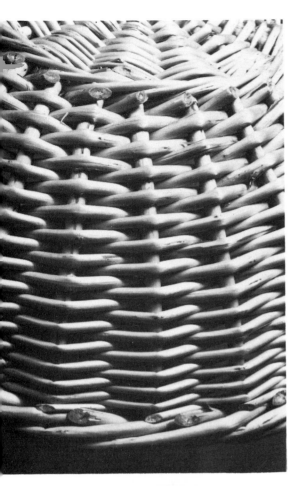

Weaving, plaiting and basket-work all have repetitive patterns, as do such household articles as graters, colanders and sieves. The soles of heavy shoes and climbing boots and tyre-treads leave patterns in mud and on roads which can give ideas for designs.

Man-made patterns frequently combine with natural ones to make yet more intricate shapes. For instance, a vine growing on a brick wall superimposes a pattern of leaf and stem shapes and their shadows on the brick background. In bright sunlight these patterns change throughout the day.

The modern embroiderer can use all of these examples and more as grist to her mill and convert them to her own use. Many of these patterns may be too complex for the beginner working alone. If you are feeling devoid of inspiration, consider the patterns produced by the window panes and decorative woodwork in such 'black and white' houses as Little Moreton Hall, Cheshire.

Enjoy your embroidery and do not make it hard work. You can begin by copying some of the patterns printed in books. Later, you may like to invent your own patterns, either on paper or directly on the fabric. Suggestions on how to do this are given in Chapter 5.

45 Man-made pattern; photograph of basket work.

46 Pattern upon pattern; a sketch of a sapling and its shadow on a brick wall.

47 Sketch of Little Moreton Hall, Cheshire.

48 Simple stitch diagrams inspired by leaded panes at Little Moreton Hall.

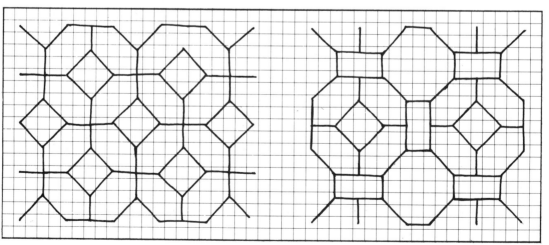

Using the patterns

Pattern for its own sake

Pattern can be used in blackwork to represent natural patterns and textures, or it may be used solely as decoration like, for example, the patterns in architecture, household objects and clothing. The chessboard in fig. 49 is a wonderful example of the purely decorative use of pattern. The whole work is a delightful piece. It is a sampler of 28 blackwork diaper patterns enclosed by a most attractive border. In Chapter 10 there are two enlargements of individual squares. The patterns are all based upon hexagons or squares, except for the royal squares. The border and the embroidered rook (castle) squares are examples of strapwork

designs, each giving the appearance of straps weaving in and out of each other.

My second example of pattern for its own sake is the detail of a tray-cloth border shown in fig. 87. The blackwork pattern used to make the border is so beautiful that I could not resist embroidering it myself on a sampler. I have also worked out on squared paper an alternative method of turning the corner. (See fig. 142.)

Making a pattern turn a corner can be quite complicated, and embroidery textbooks give detailed instructions. Marjorie Cook has cleverly avoided getting involved with diagonals and has used her basic-unit pattern the same way up all round the cloth.

The inspiration for the small sampler shown in fig. 50 came from a drawing of metal lattices used as a screen in a Chinese courtyard (D. S. Dye, *Chinese*

49 'Chessboard for Joseph', by Jennie Parry, 1980, Leicestershire. 41 cm (16¼ in.) square. Bright red linen, count 22/2.5 cm (1 in.), embroidered in black perlé, and a small amount of gold lurex in the royal squares. The patterns are based upon squares or hexagons and are not repeated except on the royal squares.

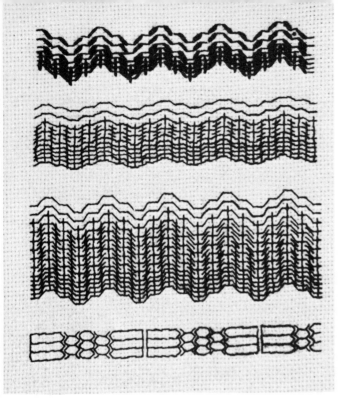

50 Sampler inspired by Chinese lattices. Off-white synthetic fabric, count 24/2.5 cm (1 in.), embroidered in black no. 40 crochet cotton and thick silk thread.

51 'Picton Castle', by Sara Woods, 1984, London College of Fashion; tutor, Anthea Godfrey. Size 25 × 20 cm (10 × 8 in.). White linen, count 24/2.5 cm (1 in.). Various thicknesses of black threads are used. The patterns fill areas of stonework. There is no outlining; each pattern is sufficiently distinct, and does not merge with the next. Some background fabric has been left plain.

Lattice Designs, Dover Publications, New York, 1974). I have used it purely for pattern and have added more and more lines from top to bottom of each sample. A three-dimensional rippling effect is created which is enhanced in the top embroidery by using two very different thicknesses of silk thread on alternate stitches. This is a favourite trick of mine. I stitch alternate stitches in one direction, and return with another thickness of thread filling in the vacant spaces completing the line (see fig. 41). Another small, simple lattice from *Chinese Lattice Designs* is embroidered at the bottom in sewing cotton.

Patterns used for specific effect

In contrast to using pattern for its own sake, in fig. 51 several diaper patterns are used to depict the stonework of a castle. In the same way, Yvette Douglas has used several different patterns in the tail feathers of a humming bird (fig. 52).

The two words pattern and design are very closely linked, and have many nuances. In this book, pattern means a repeating motif (generally small) denoting texture and other properties of the shapes which make up the over-all design. Design in the next chapter means a preliminary drawing or collage which will be the basis for an embroidery. Blackwork designs consist of shapes which are either filled on the fabric with blackwork patterns or are left unembroidered.

52 Detail of 'Humming Bird', by Yvette Douglas, Norwich; tutor, Jeannette Durrant. A variety of stitch patterns are used to create a feathery effect. The fabric is light natural linen, count 30/2.5 cm (1 in.).

3. Design

The ideas in the mind of the embroiderer for a piece of work are often very nebulous. If they are ever to reach the stitching stage, they must first be crystallized and put down on paper. The next stage is to produce a good design.

Like most artistic terms, good design and bad design are subjective and hard to define. Design is a means of communication between the artist and the viewer. The artist must use her design to convey what she wants to say. The design comes first and if it is unsatisfactory, only radical surgery can rescue a piece of work after the stitching has been done. A good design can be ruined by the use of inappropriate stitching or by bad technique, but in my experience it is more often the reverse that happens: however good the stitchery, the effect is ruined if the design is poor.

In this chapter I give some of the important points to be considered when designing.

Tones

Maurice de Sausmarez, in his book *Basic Design: The Dynamics of Visual Form*, says of tone: 'It is the quality of brightness, light and dark.'

Constance Howard, in *Inspiration for Embroidery*, says, 'Tone implies a variation between light and dark, and is a means by which interest is given to a three dimensional object or a flat surface.' In a polychromatic medium, a mood or atmosphere can be created by the choice of colours and/or tones. In a monochromatic medium, especially black, change and variety of tone are even more important.

There are an infinite number of tones between pure black and white, all of which can be called grey; when arranged in order they make a tonal scale. Greys are made in paints by mixing black and white in graded proportions. If a colour such as red is mixed with black, another series of tones is obtained. It is often difficult to decide whether a red has the same tone as another colour. But when we are dealing only with greys it is much easier to decide on their positions in the tonal scale.

In blackwork all these tones of grey are made by covering the background fabric with a varying amount of black stitching. To obtain a light tone, a thin thread and an openwork pattern is used. For a dark tone, a thick thread and a close pattern is used.

Balance of the design

All pictures must end somewhere and are therefore enclosed by a frame, real or imagined. When a shape is drawn within this frame, more shapes are produced between it and the sides of the frame. The proportions of all these shapes have been of interest to artists from earliest times. It is a vast subject. Stated in very simple terms, when a drawing is made, the blank areas on the paper are as important as the covered areas. Many students put too small an object in the middle of a large space (fig. 56(a)). This makes it lose its importance and it looks lonely. Let your shape fill the designing area and even overspill as in fig. 56(b). Usually, several shapes are used and they can overlap, creating still more shapes as in figs 57 and 58.

A good sense of balance comes with experience. It depends upon the size of the shapes and where they occur in the overall picture. Dark areas are most prominent and a small dark area may balance a larger, lighter one. Large dark areas are generally better in the lower half of the picture. The focal point of a picture is often very light or very dark and

53 Tonal scale; white to black through four shades of grey.

54 'Prisoner of Conscience', by Peggy Northen, 1984, Woking Adult Education Centre; tutor, Pamela Watts. 14×10 cm ($5\frac{1}{2} \times 4$ in.). Coarse hessian, count 20/2.5 cm (1 in.). The prison bars are in gold fingering. Note the tonal gradation obtained by varying the thicknesses of the threads and condensing the diaper patterns. The dove is outlined with a couched black thread, and left unembroidered, as in Assisi work.

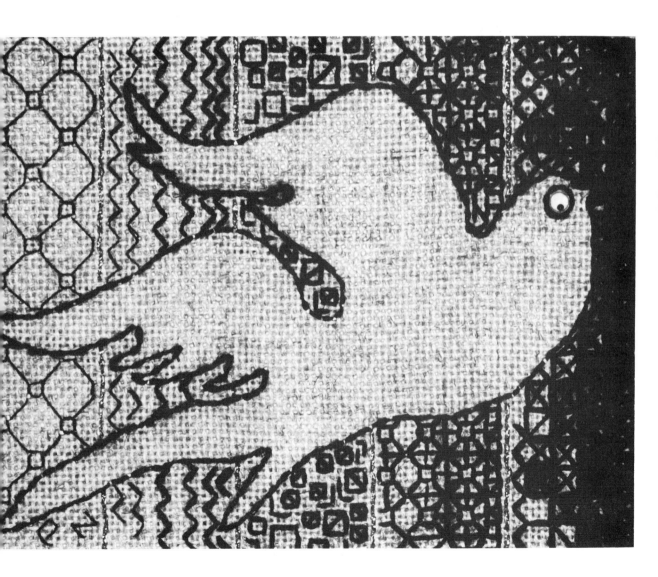

55 Design for a burse by Kathleen Lunnon, 1982, Hampton School of Needlework; tutor, Betty Sankey. 23 cm (9in.) square. White linen, count 24/2.5 cm (1 in.), embroidered with black silk. Note the dramatic tonal variety produced by different diaper patterns, and by varying the thicknesses of thread. The abstract shapes are well defined by clever use of contrast, obviating any need to outline. This is a piece of modern ecclesiastical embroidery but the diaper patterns are rooted in the sixteenth century. Note the pomegranates, and compare fig. 21.

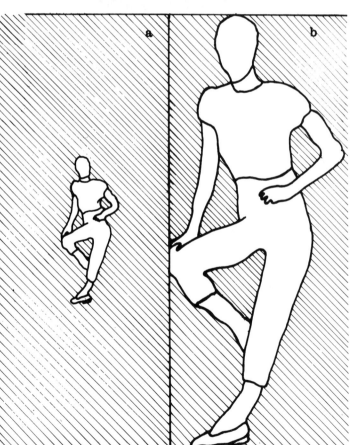

56(a) Small isolated figure.
(b) The same figure overfilling the frame and creating new, interesting areas. Derived from the panel 'Activity' by Daphne Nicholson. (See back cover.)

57 Sketch by Daphne Nicholson, Worcestershire, of overlapping figures creating even more shapes.

58 Design produced by placing a maple leaf on a sheet of paper and spraying with aerosol paint. The leaf was repositioned, overlapping the first position, and the spraying repeated. The design was closely framed to create more shapes.

59 'Eggs', by Pauline Mackenzie, 1983, Godalming Adult Education Centre; tutor, Vicky Lugg. 15 × 13 cm (6 × 5 in.). Embroidered with varying thicknesses of black threads on hessian, count 20/2.5 cm (1 in.). Two layers of black net are used to depict the shadow. Note the related shapes, overlapping and creating new shapes between themselves and the frame. The whole looks right, it is balanced.

60 'Pears', by Caroline Brailey, 1983, Godalming Adult Education Centre; tutor, Vicky Lugg. 19 cm (7½ in.) diameter. Hessian, count 20/2.5 cm (1 in.). In a small piece of work she has created good contrasting tones, by using four black threads, from medium to thick, on the coarse fabric. Much of the background is left uncovered to give the lightest tone. Because the fabric is natural hessian, the tonal scale starts at, say, number 2 on the tonal scale of fig. 53. Therefore to get adequate contrast the darkest tone needs to be a full black, and this she has made by using a Florentine stitch which covers the fabric; see also the black areas of fig. 55.

unless you especially want symmetry it should not be right in the centre.

Variety

Variety in tone, shape and area is very important. Lack of variety in tone in particular makes a dull picture. A design without tone will be difficult to 'read' from a distance. Good contrasts create vitality and drama as they do in writing, music and other disciplines.

The background is usually the lightest tone and should not be obscured unnecessarily; you did not choose it in order to cover it completely. Although

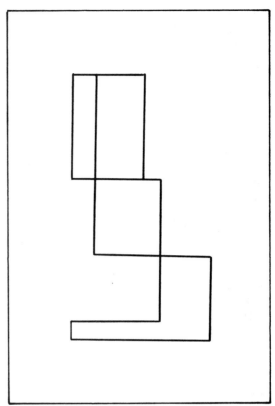

62 Rectangles which can be filled with diaper patterns in varied tones.

61 'Construction Workers' by Cecille Forgan, 1984, Hertfordshire. 20 × 10 cm (8 × 4 in.). White linen, count 20/2.5 cm (1 in.). The design was inspired by a newspaper photograph which needed little adaptation. A large proportion of background is left clear, adding to the impression of men working at a height. The men are embroidered with black perlé satin stitch.

variety of tone is very important, too much variety in shape can be disturbing and can detract from the overall effect.

When planning a design, it is best to think of it as shapes or areas, not as lines. Lines make the shapes which are to be filled with stitches. Large, medium and small areas of related shapes are best for the beginner. Some very interesting designs have been made by combining squares and rectangles of various sizes and filling each with a distinct tone. Combinations of squares and rectangles with irregular triangles and other shapes can be tricky. Shapes help to express the mood. Sharp, acute angles give a feeling of chaos and jerky movement, whereas gentle curves have a calming effect.

Unless a very fine linen is used, most stitch patterns will not fit into the shape made by a very acute angle and embroidering will be difficult. Also, very small shapes are not practical when using any counted-thread technique. This will be dealt with in Chapter 6. However, when designing, several small shapes can often be blended together.

63 'Pear', by Rae Knight, 1970s, Malden Adult Education Centre; tutor, Margaret Pascoe. 22 × 13 cm (8½ × 5 in.). Medium-fine linen, varied black threads; diaper patterns in overlapping rectangles (see Fig. 62). The pear outlining is a couched black wool thread, and the pips are 'sprats' heads' done with a very thick thread. The design was taken from a conté crayon drawing in *Blackwork Embroidery* by Geddes and McNeill. This method is akin to a line and wash picture. It gives just an impression of the object portrayed. (*Photograph, Annie Strugnell.*)

a

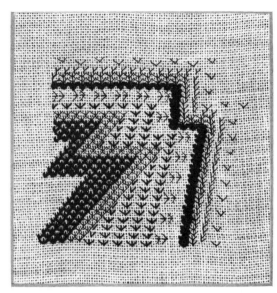

b

65 Sampler by Patricia Broughall, 1983, Godalming Adult Education Centre; tutor, Vicky Lugg. 13 cm (5 in.) square. The idea for the design came from the eaves of Little Moreton Hall (see fig. 47). Off-white linen, count 20/2.5 cm (1 in.). The angles suggest movement.

64 Chaotic angles, conveying agitation, lack of comfort, hostility. A drawing was made of sharp angles unrelated to each other. These made jagged shapes between the lines. The drawing was traced on to the back of a piece of black adhesive paper, and the shapes cut out carefully with a sharp knife. (a) was made by sticking down some of the shapes on to a square of white paper. (b) is the negative of (a) and was made by using the left-over shapes from (a). The packs of coloured adhesive papers sold for childrens' craft work generally contain black and other dark toned papers which work equally well.

66 A tranquil design composed of flowing curves. (*Photograph (by Rosemary Weller) of the copyright design 'Tranquillity' and Shape 225, reproduced with the kind permission of Josiah Wedgwood & Sons Ltd of Barlaston, Stoke-on-Trent, England. © Josiah Wedgwood & Sons Ltd 1985.*)

55

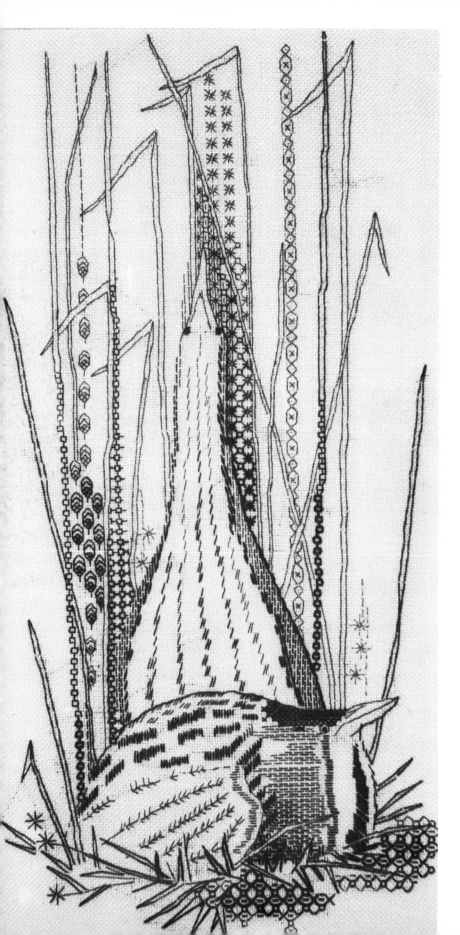

67 'Bitterns', by Jenny Chippindale, 1984, London College of Fashion; tutor, Anthea Godfrey. 29 × 15 cm (11½ × 6 in.). White evenweave fabric, count 30/ 2.5 cm (1 in.), delicately embroidered in the manner of a pen and ink sketch, using fine black threads. There are no strong outlines. The birds merge into the reeds as they do in nature.

68 'Wimbledon High Street', by Roni Karlsen, 1983, Merton Adult Education Centre; tutor, Hilary Cooper. 20 × 15 cm (8 × 6 in.). White linen, count 28/2.5 cm (1 in.) embroidered with varied thicknesses of black silk. In the design the road leads the eye into the picture.

Outlines can be made definite or they can fade into the background. In modern work an added outline is not often used, but at one time it was considered essential. Where lines are required to complete a design they can be added by couching a thread.

You will now see that a pleasing arrangement of simple shapes of differing sizes and tones is required. Most subjects can be simplified into such an arrangement; for example, architectural features such as roofs, walls, doors and gateways are shapes which can be filled with pattern (fig. 68). Natural objects such as leaves, trees and bushes can also be used in this way. Each shape has its own texture or pattern (fig. 72).

Methods of designing

Drawing or painting

If you can draw or paint you can start with a picture of your own which can be simplified into shapes.

57

69 'St Paul's Cathedral', by Heather Maton, 1984, West Hampshire and Dorset Branch of the Embroiderers' Guild. Size 15 × 24 cm (6 × 9½ in.) on a synthetic evenweave fabric, count 24/2.5 cm (1 in.). A complicated subject well simplified. Note the use of half hexagons in the church spire on the right, over four threads at the base and over two threads at the top. The dome is covered with a black hexagonal net.

70 'Christchurch Priory', by Dorothy Cook, 1984, West Hampshire and Dorset Branch of the Embroiderers' Guild. Size 20 × 25 cm (8 × 10 in.), on linen, count 20/2.5 cm (1 in.). Some gold threads are used on the tree on the left. There is good contrast in the shapes of the trees and the Priory. The original inspiration was detailed and complicated, but a simple effective interpretation, suitable for blackwork, has been achieved.

71 'Brighton Pavilion', by Gladys Nancarrow, 1984,
West Hampshire and Dorset Branch of the Embroiderers' Guild. Size 32 × 39 cm (12½ × 15 in.) on a loosely
woven white linen, count 28/2.5 cm (1 in.). This is light
airy treatment for a large building, with good interest in
the balustrade in the foreground.

72 'Mountain Scene', by Pamela Fraser, 1970s, New Malden Adult Education Centre; tutor, Margaret Pascoe. Fabric, white linen. This piece was nearly all designed on the final fabric, with the use of a small stitch sampler for the trees. Each tree has its own individual pattern. (*Photograph, Annie Strugnell.*)

Drawing with the side of a piece of charcoal, a pastel or a conté crayon on a rough-surfaced paper is particularly suitable for blackwork. In these media, hard outlines are softened and textured shapes evolve spontaneously. Detailed shading is not necessary.

You may be one of the many embroiderers who feel that they cannot draw, and that any attempt to commit a subject to paper is a waste of time. However, the very act of drawing or painting combines hand and eye and this helps you to become much more familiar with the subject you are depicting, than you would by just looking at it.

Spraying

Cardboard shapes and small objects such as leaves or clothes pegs are placed on a large sheet of paper. Paint is sprayed around these. If the objects are

73   Pen and ink drawing by Daphne Nicholson, 1982.

moved and the paper resprayed, a design is produced with interesting shapes and tones as in fig. 58.

Photographs

Many embroiderers dislike drawing but can adapt a photograph. I find the black-and-white sections in photographic exhibitions a great source of inspiration. The best examples are those that catch your eye when entering the room and which when examined in detail give marvellous ideas for pattern and texture. In such pictures the three-dimensional objects are already turned into two-dimensional shapes, and the photographer will have given much thought to composing a pleasing design.

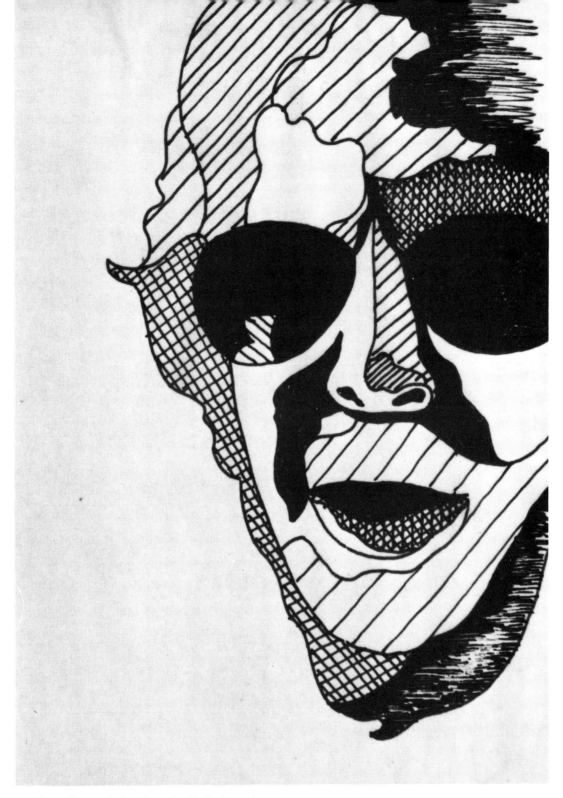

74 Tone diagram derived from fig. 73. Each tonal area
is outlined and the tone represented by shading, or
hatching. A total of six tonal values are used.

75 'Sandy', by Daphne Nicholson, 1982, Worcester-shire. 13 × 18 cm (5 × 7 in.). Natural linen, count 26/2.5 cm (1 in.), mostly black embroidery threads with some grey Anchor stranded thread used in hair and nose to lighten the tone. Anchor soft embroidery thread is used at the edge of the beard.

76 Newspaper picture of a hang-glider. Very little modification would be needed for interpretation in embroidery. The tonal areas are clearly defined and are not too numerous. Note the close framing of the subject.

Photographs and diagrams in technical journals can suggest designs because they often have strong definitive and unusual shapes. Similarly, photographs in newspapers, magazines and posters already have defined tone values, and will have been composed to produce maximum visual impact. In many cases the pictures need simplifying by reducing the number of tones and/or shapes. In the beginning, it is best to keep to three tones, and

certainly not more than five. Certain newspaper pictures are almost ready to use because the printing process automatically reduces the range of tones. Some pictures in advertisements have excessive contrast to catch the eye, and little if any further simplication is required. Others are made using a photographic technique known as posterization, whereby highlights are white, shadows are black, and the rest is a uniform grey (fig. 77).

Paper collage

After tracing off the main shapes in a picture, I cut them out from black and grey papers and stick them

65

77 Tone diagram using only three tones, made with black, grey and white sugar paper; inspired by pastel self portrait of Maurice Quentin de la Tour. In interpreting such a diagram, some intermediate tones can be added to soften the contrast where it is excessive, such as on the face.

78 Area diagram using only black and white. This was derived from an X-ray of a shell, and forms the basis of the embroidery in fig. 123, using the four lower white shapes.

down on to a white background. A cheaper method is to select newspaper cuttings of various tonal values. These have an added advantage because the print may suggest textures and directions for the stitchery. Newspaper collage is an art in its own right and used as an aid in designing, helps you to criticize your picture. Do not hurry over this. You may be eager to start stitching, but time is well spent at this stage and a good design will save mistakes later which may be costly in time and material.

Abstract designs can be quickly made by pasting down cut or torn white tissue paper on to black sugar paper. Highlights can be added with white poster paint. It is easy to translate these tissue-paper collages into black stitching on a light ground (fig. 83).

Before using your design, make a negative of it. There is no need to do this photographically; simply make a new collage with the tonal values reversed. Sometimes the shapes shown up in the negative are more interesting than those in the original. This is exploited in the form of embroidery known as Assisi work; see figs 54 and 125 for a similar effect using blackwork.

The whole of your collage or drawing may not be needed. The use of a viewing frame – a rectangular hole in a piece of card – or 'L' masks to select the

79 Newspaper picture, top left, and derivation from it using newspaper collage, by Peggy Northen. See fig. 54 for its interpretation in blackwork.

80 Drawing by Sylvia Drinkwater of five ladies under an umbrella.

81 Newspaper collage derived from fig. 80. The added
ink lines give emphasis.

a

82 Positive and negative shapes combined to make an abstract design. A lid to a plastic egg carton depicted two lines of hens boldly silhouetted. (a) depicts the original label. Two tracings were made from the label; in one the hens were painted black, and in the second the background was painted black. The two patterns were then joined together with the hens' legs in register, and the design cropped to produce (b).

As an abstract design, it can be used up, down or sideways. In translating the design into embroidery, the theme of domestic fowls could be retained by suitable stitching, perhaps to suggest feathers; or the original source could be forgotten and the shapes interpreted as they appeal to the embroiderer. A further abstraction can be made by not keeping to the original black and white idea but by transposing black and white randomly, thus getting further away from the original source.

b

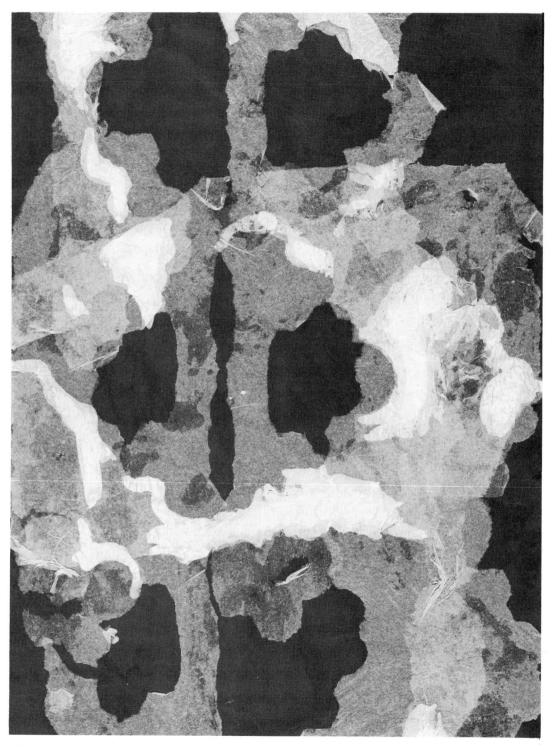

83 Abstract design in tissue-paper collage, on black
sugar paper with white poster paint added for emphasis.

most interesting part of your design is very helpful (fig. 78). In any case, draw a rectangular frame around the design to mark its limits.

Turn your collage picture upside down, view it from all sides, prop it up somewhere you pass frequently, and you may find that alterations suggest themselves. Never decide on a design without seeing it from a distance. Look at it in a mirror, which will double the apparent distance and also reverse the design. Give yourself a break and then look at it again; you may get new ideas. Too much concentration at one sitting is not good. Do not be afraid to ask for opinions from your friends. You may not take their advice, but it will make you reconsider your design.

Keep all your preliminary designs, at least until the embroidery is finished. If at any time the needlework becomes difficult, you can then look back at your original ideas. Ask yourself if you have forgotten the objectives? What has been lost? Is it possible to recapture it, or has some better design been suggested in translating from paper to fabric?

I must emphasize that the points mentioned in this chapter are *aids* to design, not hard and fast rules. They can be ignored deliberately in order to get a specific effect; for example, a little figure walking in a large, featureless expanse may purposely be used to suggest loneliness.

There are many more methods for deriving designs than I have been able to describe in this chapter. There is a ferment of experimentation in this aspect of art, and new methods are being used all the time. Practical-study courses are held in various locations. Why not see what is available in your area? Courses aimed directly at embroiderers are advertised by the Embroiderers' Guild.

4. Materials and tools

In recent years embroidery has opened up to combine with other media. Nowadays, the background fabric can be painted or sprayed with dyes, and pieces of ceramics, paper, and so on, can be included. In surface embroidery, many novelty threads – bouclés, mohair, etc. – are used to produce textures with long stitches which are raised above the surface of the background fabric and sometimes hang free. These techniques do not appeal to all embroiderers and some prefer a method such as blackwork which directly involves the structure of the fabric. The detailed formal stitching over counted threads and the repeating patterns based on a fixed network can be relaxing and soothing.

Previous chapters have illustrated examples from the past, introduced the small geometrical patterns on which the technique is based, and explained how to design a piece of work. Now you have to find your fabric, frames, needles, threads, scissors and get to work.

Fabric

This is very important. There can be no embroidery without a background fabric. Weavers and lacemakers make their own, but embroiderers must choose a fabric. Usually for blackwork embroidery the background is white or natural-linen colour, and is the same shade throughout. A painted or printed background can be used, but this will be dealt with later (page 115).

An evenweave fabric is essential; this means one with a plain weave, in which the threads of the warp and weft are identical and are of equal diameter along their length. The shuttle carrying the weft yarn goes over one warp thread and under the next for one throw, and reverses the movement for the next. The yarns used are flax (linen), jute (hessian), cotton, wool and synthetics, alone or mixed. Linens frequently have slubs but these should be as few as possible. There is much less likelihood of slubs in cotton materials.

Linen is a beautiful and enduring material, but top-grade linens are very expensive. For most purposes one can use a slightly imperfect quality, which is cheaper. This will probably have more slubs and in a very fine piece of work these could distort the blackwork patterns. For less fine work and samplers it is perfectly adequate.

The count, that is, the number of threads per centimetre or per inch, should be the same in both warp and weft; this is what makes fabric an evenweave. When buying evenweave material, remember that a larger count means a finer fabric. Personally, I find a count greater than 30 threads per 2.5 cm (1 in.) too fine to see easily without the use of a magnifying glass. If the fabric is bought at a needlework shop, the count will be marked on the label. Sometimes the count is expressed in *holes* per 2.5 cm (1 in.).

The fabric should be sufficiently closely woven so that it is not transparent. If the threads are too widely spaced as in gauze or scrim, it is difficult to make the embroidered pattern show up, and the threads on the back show through. Openweave fabrics, such as scrim, can be used for specific effects; because of their transparent nature it is necessary to choose a suitable backing material when mounting the finished work.

Some furnishing fabrics such as hopsacks and hessian are easy to work on, and are available in beautiful colours. These are worth searching for in

84 Needlebook, 'Prospect of Norwich', by Jenny Daniels, 1984, Norwich; tutor, Jeanette Durrant. 11.5 × 9 cm (4½ × 3½ in.). White linen, count 30/2.5 cm (1 in.) with black silk embroidery, tassel and cord in black perlé. Small motif and similar border on the back.

a   b   c

d   e   f

85 Evenweave linens suitable for blackwork. (a) to (f) are photographs of linens through a mask of 2.5 cm (1 in.) square. Thus the number of threads along a side of a square is the count of the material. If the count is the same in both directions, the linen is called evenweave.

(a) Count 31/2.5 cm (1 in.). A large slub can be seen slightly left of centre.

(b) Count 26/2.5 cm (1 in.). Note the large slub. (a) and (b) were sold as 'slightly imperfect evenweave linens'.

(c) Count 19/2.5 cm (1 in.). This is a good-quality linen with most of the threads equal in diameter.

(d) Count 33/2.5 cm (1 in.). An almost similar count to (a), but better quality.

(e) Count 17/2.5 cm (1 in.). This is a coarse, heavy fabric and has a dark natural linen colour. It would be very hard wearing and was used for protective clothing, such as aprons, in former times. This fabric would clearly not be suitable for delicate stitching.

(f) Count 42/2.5 cm (1 in.). This linen is woven from very uneven yarn. It would be difficult to embroider, particularly in places where two sets of slubs coincided.

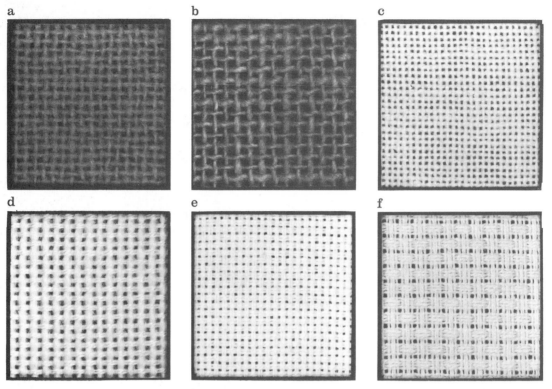

86 (a) Count 16/2.5 cm (1 in.). A soft, pale-blue wool flannel. It is easy to work on and worth searching for in the shops.
(b) Count 14/2.5 cm (1 in.). A synthetic furnishing fabric, beige in colour. This works well with a thick embroidery thread.
(c) Count 26/2.5 cm (1 in.). A cotton evenweave, and free from slubs.
(d) A synthetic/wool hopsack. It has a count of 18 double-weave synthetic threads × 16 woollen ones. The difference in the counts does not seem to affect the stitch patterns greatly, and I have used this fabric extensively for the examples of stitch patterns in this book. As far as I know, it is not available now.

(e) Count 22/2.5 cm (1 in.) in both directions. This is Hardanger, a double evenweave, cotton fabric used for the Norwegian counted-thread technique of the same name. The fabric is very even and smooth.
(f) Aida fabric. A complex weave in which the holes are prominent; count 10 (holes)/2.5 cm (1 in.). It is also available with higher counts. This kind of weave prevents the embroidery stitches lying close together. Therefore the generation of different tonal areas is difficult, and the fabric is more suitable for pattern-making rather than panels.

the curtain-fabric department of a store. They will not be marked with the count, but with experience you will be able to judge by eye what will be suitable for you. Fabrics with different warp and weft yarns and slightly differing counts each way make interesting backgrounds for experienced workers, but I would not recommend them to beginners.

When buying a fabric, be sure that the assistant cuts it along the weft. Ideally, before cutting, a thread should be pulled to show the line of the weave. Remnants can be bargains but may not be

cut along the weave, so you may be getting less material than you think. Figs 87–91 show some of the variety of fabrics which can be used for black-work; see also figs 54, 59 and 60 for the use of hessian.

Frames

Some embroiderers produce beautiful work on a piece of fabric held loose in the hand. If you are used to doing this for other embroidery techniques,

87 An exceptionally fine natural linen, count 44/2.5 cm (1 in.). A traycloth by Marjorie Cook, 1960s, Hertfordshire, Royal School of Needlework. Embroidered in black filoselle silk and a small amount of gold thread. See also Chapters 2 and 10.

88 Coarse natural linen, count 20/2.5 cm (1 in.). 'Arches', by Eileen Plumridge, 1984, Woking Adult Education Centre; tutor, Pamela Watts. 20 × 13 cm (8 × 5 in.). Embroidered with various black threads. Design derived from a drawing by Wyndham Lewis of Edith Sitwell.

continue to do so. Personally, I find framing the fabric, so that it is taut and stretched squarely, a great advantage. The woven yarns of the fabric are held at right-angles so that the finished work is not askew, and a frame can be fixed so that you have both hands free to sew with. When a piece of work is in progress it is important to assess it continually, looking at it from a distance and from all angles. A picture looks very different when hung rather than lying flat on the table. A framed fabric can be propped up in various places, but unframed work

77

89 Hardanger fabric, plain-weave cotton with double warp and weft yarns, count 22 holes/2.5 cm (1 in.). This fabric has an extremely regular and close weave; see also figs 27 and 122.

Detail from 'Houses by the Canal in Bruges', by Kay Bews, 1983, Reading Adult Education Centre; tutor, Jean Mould. The embroidery was mounted on card, and then stuck on to a calico-covered background. The patterns were in fine silky threads of various colours. The prominent barge boards are of applied black kid.

must be pinned and repinned to the detriment of the fabric and with loss of time.

Three types of frames are used in embroidery: tambour, slate and canvas stretchers.

Tambour frames

Circular or tambour frames are the type familiar to viewers of classic serials on the television, in which the lady of the house sits at her needlework. They consist of double wooden or metal hoops fitting one inside the other. The outer hoop is provided with a means of tightening so as to grip the fabric between it and the inner hoop.

It is advisable to bind the inner hoop with tape or bias binding as this allows the fabric to be gripped better and kept cleaner. Tambour frames are sold in a range of sizes, some quite large, and can be obtained with clamps to fasten them to the edge of a table so that both hands are free. Dressing, or stretching the fabric on the frame, is easiest with a tambour, but slate or stretcher frames are kinder to the fabric. Pinching the fabric between the hoops of the tambour can distort the weave permanently, and can leave an unwanted and visually disturbing circular mark around the finished embroidery. Several of the embroideries illustrated in this book suffered from this fault.

I use a small tambour frame, 10 cm (4 in.) in diameter, for trying out samples of stitches before

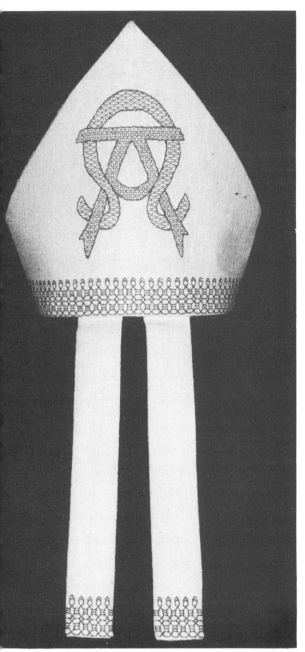

90 Cream slubbed cotton furnishing fabric, count 24/ 2.5 cm (1 in.). The slubs are small and so do not intrude upon the patterns, but they do add interest to the fabric.

Mitre, back view (photographed by kind permission of the Right Rev. Michael Adie, the Lord Bishop of Guildford). Designed and made by Barbara Thomson, 1983, London. Embroidered in grey Anchor stranded cotton. The alpha and omega motif is outlined in whipped running stitch. An outline is needed in this instance to make the motif clear from a distance. The front of the mitre is similar to the back.

91 Coarse evenweave, brown wool tweed dress fabric. 'Boy's Head', by Edna Messam, 1982, Merton Adult Education Centre; tutor, Hilary Cooper. Count 16/2.5 cm (1 in.); 25×16.5 cm ($10 \times 6\frac{1}{2}$ in.). Commissioned for the Embroiderers' Guild *Blackwork Study Folio*, 1984. Design derived from an educational magazine photograph, inset bottom.

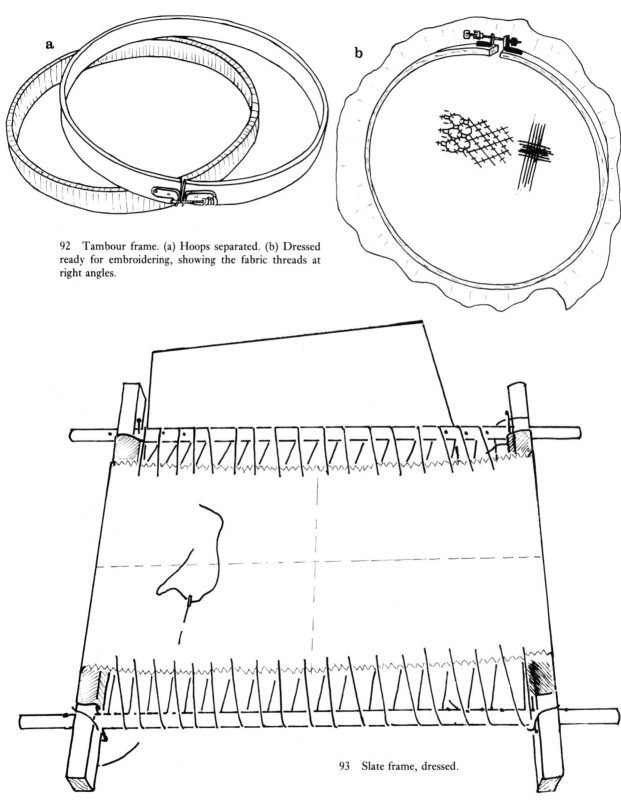

92   Tambour frame. (a) Hoops separated. (b) Dressed ready for embroidering, showing the fabric threads at right angles.

93   Slate frame, dressed.

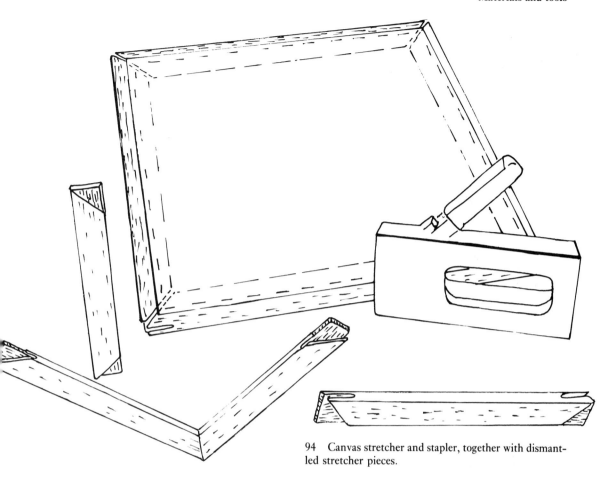

94 Canvas stretcher and stapler, together with dismantled stretcher pieces.

using them on the embroidery proper, for which I use a slate frame.

Slate frames

Slate frames are available in many different designs, some unnecessarily complicated and expensive, though works of art in themselves. Basically, all that is needed are two rollers to which the fabric is attached. These rollers are kept apart, putting the fabric under tension, by two side pieces known as stretchers. The way the rollers are attached to the stretchers must be such that the resultant frame is a true rectangle.

The fabric is sewn to pieces of webbing permanently fixed to the rollers. The distance apart of the rollers can be varied to adjust the tension in the fabric and to accommodate different sizes of work. The fabric is stretched in the other direction by lacing to the stretchers. The length of the webbing attached to the rollers decides the maximum width of work that can be accommodated on the frame, and frames are sold according to this length. For a beginner I would recommend a 45 cm (18 in.) frame.

Canvas stretchers

These are used by artists for stretching their canvases and can be obtained from art shops. In my view they are not as suitable for blackwork embroidery as slate frames. A frame is made up from four wooden stretchers. These are sold in pairs in a variety of lengths so that one can make rectangles of different proportions.

Embroidery threads

Blackwork uses a smooth thread, that is, it is of even

diameter throughout the skein. Traditionally, the colour of the thread is always in contrast to that of the background fabric.

There are many black threads, and they may be made of cotton, silk, wool, linen or synthetics. There are too many on the market to list them all here. In your first piece it is best to restrict the number of different threads you use. Personally I would recommend three in order of thickness, starting with the thinnest:

1 No. 50 cotton or silk sewing thread.
2 Buttonhole silk number 40/3, or Polytwist by Gütermann.
3 No. 5 perlé cotton.

These are for use on a fabric with a count of between 8 and 10 threads per cm (20 to 25 threads per in.).

Thinner cotton threads, particularly those used for machine embroidery, and lace threads, give a precise, delicate stitch. There are also available varying thicknesses of silk threads from number 200/3 (finest), to 10/3. The number 3 refers to the ply, i.e. the number of strands that are twisted together to make the thread. In embroidery threads, three-ply is most usual, but you may also meet two-ply. On more openweave fabrics, thicker perlés, crochet cottons, cotons à broder, and Anchor or DMC soft embroidery threads can be used. I recommend that beginners use recognized embroidery threads. Later, when they have gained experience, they may wish to experiment with threads made for other purposes. One thing to look for when choosing such a thread is that it is not too springy; if it is, the stitches will not lie properly on the fabric, and the straight lines which are so characteristic of blackwork will be impossible to achieve.

Crewel wool and darning wool are good for dark areas in a design; their slightly fuzzy quality obscures the underlying fabric. When using threads from different manufacturers in the same piece of work, check that they are all of the same shade. Some threads which are not as black as others look rusty or dark brown and do not mix well with true blacks.

Amongst the great variety of threads which are available, you will find that some are dull and matt, others will have a slight sheen and others again will be definitely shiny, with a pronounced twist. All these properties can be used to give specific effects in your work.

Many embroiderers use Anchor or DMC stranded cotton, which is composed of six threads. To obtain different thicknesses of line they use from one to six at a time in the needle. I do not recommend this. A single thread of stranded cotton soon becomes fuzzy when stitching. If a fine line is needed, I prefer a fine sewing thread; this wears better both in the needle and on the fabric. For thicker lines, I prefer to use a thicker, twisted yarn. Using more than one thread at a time in the needle does not produce such a good line since the individual threads are apt to pull differently, producing loops.

Interesting contrasts can be made by using a white or light-coloured thread on a dark background, not necessarily white on black since black linen is difficult to count and may soil the white thread. If you feel that black on white embroidery is restricting, this adaptation is a fertile field to explore.

Gold thread

It is traditional to use gold threads in blackwork. In my view a small amount of gold goes a long way. A lavish use of gold may be ostentatious, an adjective that does not blend happily with blackwork.

A fine passing thread (obtainable from metal-thread specialist suppliers) is best, and great care must be taken with this when pulling to avoid distorting the weave. It is difficult to pull such a thread through a *fine* linen and couching the gold thread on the surface with a matching silk is an alternative method.

The best gold threads are very expensive but they never tarnish. The gold chain stitch in the Elizabethan motif illustrated in fig. 15 is as bright as ever. Cheaper 'gold' threads are available but except for the new synthetics, they quickly tarnish. Lurex and similar synthetic 'metal' threads are readily available and can be used discreetly with good effect.

Durability of fabrics and threads

The collectors' pieces of embroidery have survived because they were made using the best materials. If you want your work to last, as you might if it is an ecclesiastical embroidery, choose your fabrics and threads carefully. Linen is still the ideal fabric for blackwork, and silk is probably the best thread. These have stood the test of time.

There is no way of knowing the life of modern fibres; only time will tell. Methods such as painting and spraying the fabric may also produce problems. However, do not let this discourage you from experimenting. No art should attempt to stand still or it will die. We must use the exciting new materials of our own time as well as the older, time-

95 A 1960s sampler, embroiderer unknown. The embroidery is original and bold and reminiscent of sixteenth-century blackwork. The gold knots are embroidered with several strands in the needle. This piece is in the Embroiderers Guild *Blackwork Study Folio*, 1984.

proven ones. In any case, for the most part we embroider for our own enjoyment, and not with an eye to posterity.

Needles

These should be tapestry needles, that is, fairly thick needles with long eyes and blunt points. A sharp-pointed needle such as a chenille or crewel needle will more easily split the threads of the fabric and this must be avoided. I find that three sizes of tapestry needle, numbers 18, 22 and 26 serve for most purposes. Packets of mixed sizes of tapestry needles from numbers 18 to 24 are easily available, but for the finest work you will need number 26, which can be obtained from specialist suppliers. Sometimes a short end of thread needs to be pulled to the back of the fabric and woven into the pattern to secure it. If it is too short to use in a needle a fine metal crochet hook or needle-threader can be used to pull it through.

Scissors

A pair of small, sharp-pointed embroidery scissors is essential. These must be sharp; a blunt pair of scissors is a handicap to any embroiderer. Jealously guard your embroidery scissors. Avoid cutting coarse threads with the tips of the blades, as this quickly ruins them. Embroidery scissors are expensive, so keep a larger pair of scissors to hand for coarse work.

Thimbles

Not all needlewomen use a thimble, but it does protect your finger, and when a very large number of stitches are made it is advisable to work with one. A thimble is a personal choice, and when well used becomes an old and valued friend. For me a thimble is a must. Some embroiderers use a thimble on each hand.

Magnification

For fine work some form of magnification may be required. Those who are short-sighted are lucky in this respect – they can remove their spectacles and bring the work closer. For people with normal vision and more importantly for those who require glasses for reading, a magnifying glass can be a great help. There are many types available at a wide range of prices. Only you can tell what will suit you. Before buying anything expensive, make certain that you are happy using it. Ideally, you need something which leaves both hands free for sewing.

5. Making a sampler

Having learned something about materials and tools, you can now stitch a sampler. For this a tambour frame is useful.

Dressing a tambour frame

Cut a piece of fabric large enough to fit over the frame, leaving a border of at least 2.5 cm (1 in.) all round (fig. 92(b)). Machine or oversew round the edge to prevent fraying. Put the inner hoop of the frame on the table. Place the piece of fabric over the hoop, and press the outer hoop firmly down over the fabric. Do not force the outer hoop, but loosen the adjustment so that it is an easy fit. Now tighten it so that the fabric is held firmly. Next pull the fabric taut and square; do not overdo the tension, and look at the warp and weft to see that they are straight and square. When you are satisfied with the result, tighten the outer hoop fully.

Using a piece of evenweave fabric to dress the whole tambour in this way is extravagant for small samplers. A small piece of fabric can be used in any frame by attaching it to a larger piece of cheaper material. To do this, sew the small piece of evenweave material firmly all round the edge on to the middle of a larger piece of old sheeting or similar fabric. I use a machine and zigzag around the fabric twice, but whichever method you use must be firm. Cut away the sheeting behind the evenweave material, and dress the frame as described.

The method of dressing a slate frame is described on page 98.

You are going to stitch into the fabric through the holes between the threads, so the embroidery thread lines are governed by the construction of the fabric. It is on this grid of warp and weft that the embroidery will be worked.

The count of the fabric

The count of the fabric or, to be more precise, the size of the holes, dictates the range of thicknesses of threads to be used. Most importantly, the thread should never be so thick as to distort the weave of the fabric. At the other end of the range, too fine a thread will not lie properly in the holes and will tend to pull the fabric. Also, too fine a thread will tend to be lost on an openweave fabric. For beginners to blackwork, I suggest starting with evenweave linen, count not more than 10 threads per cm (25 per in.) and buttonhole thread no. 40/3 or no. 30/3 silk or synthetic (Polytwist, Gütermanns).

Making diaper patterns

The building bricks of any blackwork pattern are shown in fig. 96, row 1.

Holbein or double running stitch

To embroider a line on your sampler, follow the three stages in its construction in fig. 96(5).

Many embroiderers use a back stitch (fig. 96 (6)) instead, believing that it gives a straighter line. Try it for yourself and decide which method you will adopt. Of course if you wish to make your work reversible, back stitching cannot be used.

I suggest that you embroider a row of one of these basic stitches evenly spaced, and develop it as illustrated in fig. 102f. This is only a suggestion. It

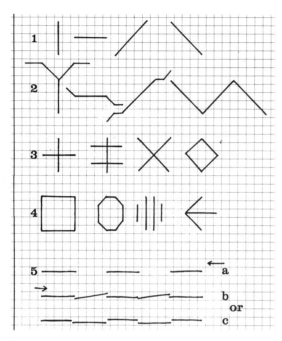

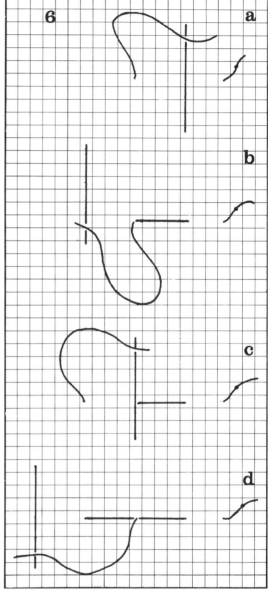

96
(1) Basic building bricks.
(2) Tree, step and zigzag stitch.
(3) & (4) Other simple stitches.
(5) Holbein stitch. (a) A row of running stitches is worked from right to left. Then either (b) or (c) is worked, generally from left to right, filling in the spaces left in (a). The slanting stitches in (b) give a better line than the straight stitches in (c). Although it may not be obvious in the diagram, all the stitches are of equal length, passing over the same number of threads in each case.
(6) Back stitch. Although the line made by the stitches begins at the right-hand end and finishes at the left-hand end, each individual stitch is sewn from left to right (i.e. backwards) and long stitches which overlap are produced on the wrong side of the fabric, from right to left.

is fun to play around with the basic bricks, building your own pattern.

Experiment further with the basic stitches; invent diaper patterns and then join them up. Try out some simple patterns following stitch diagrams, and experiment with these. In other words, familiarize yourself with stitching patterns both by inventing and copying. Perhaps at quiet moments you could get ideas by doodling on paper – it is quicker and very often more convenient than embroidering directly on the fabric. However, you must then try out your ideas either on the fabric or by making a stitch diagram on squared paper. You will find that your sketches will not always translate easily into

stitches. You must then be flexible and adapt your ideas to fit the grid of the material. You will often get new ideas in the process.

The idea for the stitching pattern in the bottom right-hand corner of fig. 98, came from a cast-iron ventilator grill in the wall of a Guernsey school. When I tried to convert my rough sketch into stitches, I found that it was not possible in the original form, but by experimenting upon squared paper this pattern evolved.

It is easiest if your stitches are made over two or

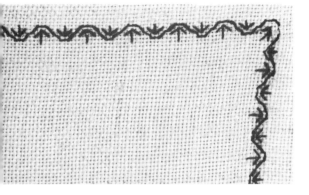

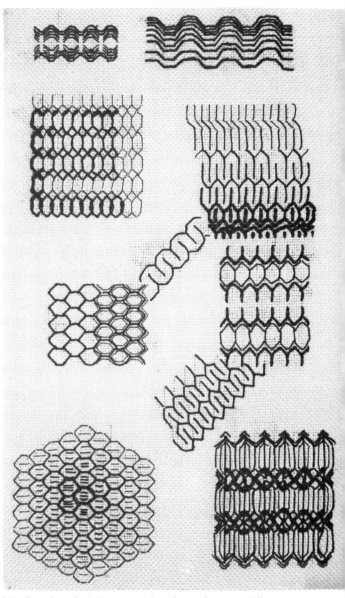

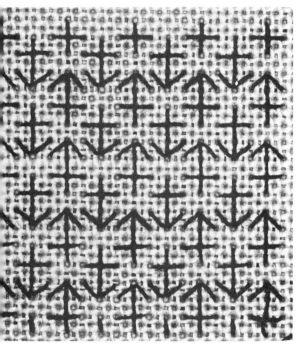

97 Two of the simplest patterns made from the building bricks. The border is from Osyth Wood's tray cloth shown in fig. 23, and the other pattern from fig. 49, 'Chessboard for Joseph'.

98 Sampler of stitch patterns based on a hexagon. All except the bottom right corner evolved on the fabric, starting from a simple hexagon or part of one.

four threads. In this way there is a central hole, and if you wish to alternate the pattern you can do so easily. The hexagon stitch illustrated in fig. 100 shows this clearly. You will soon find that if you make a stitch over only one thread, it can disappear.

If you *can* avoid coming up through a hole which already has a thread in it, do so. It is better to go down such a hole because the work will look neater this way. However, this is not always possible.

With practice you will learn the best sequence of stitches to give you an even pull; the final direction of the stitch can be tricky, especially on a loose weave. If the areas are separated from each other by more than a very short distance, do not carry a thread across from one area to another on the back of the work. It may show through the holes of the

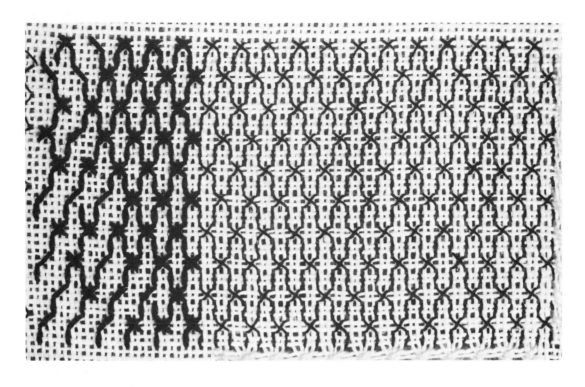

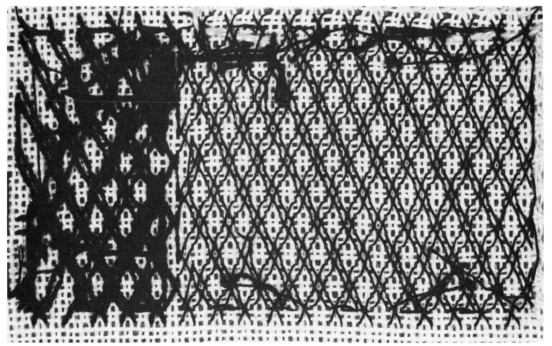

99(a) Front. (b) Back of part of the sampler shown in fig. 127. The regularity of the back threads shows a planned method of working leading to the right 'pull' of the threads on the front. Note this lattice is the basis of several patterns in the Alhambra, Granada, Spain.

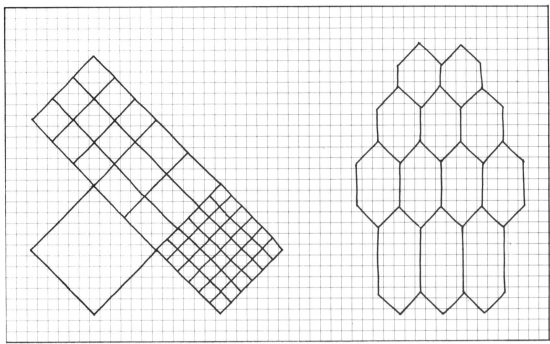

100 Stitch diagram showing an enlargement of two stitches, each over an increasing number of threads. See also fig. 102(c).

fabric. Sometimes this is not apparent until the work is mounted. This does not apply to a small sampler.

Using patterns to create tones

In Chapter 3 I refer to the importance of varied tones. I also mentioned the use of thin and thick threads and open and close patterns to make different tones. Try these ideas out on your sampler. Cross stitch in a fine thread over a minimum number of holes produces an even, black tone.

I suggest three ways of altering the tone value of a particular diaper pattern, and you should practice these before attempting a larger piece of work.

1 Stitch the pattern over two threads, over four threads, and over six threads. Use the same thickness of thread throughout. You will see that as you stitch over a larger number of threads the tone is lightened and the diaper pattern enlarges. Unless the linen is very fine, there quickly comes a limit to the enlargement of the pattern. Certainly, if the embroidery is to be handled and washed, long

threads are liable to be pulled. This may be avoided by using double running stitches to create the large patterns, but the result does not always look right.

2 Stitch the pattern over the same number of threads each time but use a thinner embroidery thread as you progress. I suggest:

> one row perlé no. 5
> one row perlé no. 8
> one row buttonhole silk or synthetic
> one row Sylko no. 40.

See figs 102 d and e, 103.

3 Stitch the pattern over the same number of threads each time, but take away part of the pattern progressively (fig. 102a).

Of course, you can use combinations of the three methods, but beware of making your work too complicated.

Varying the pattern randomly within an area

It is not always best to embroider the same pattern evenly over a whole area. In Chapter 2, I pointed out

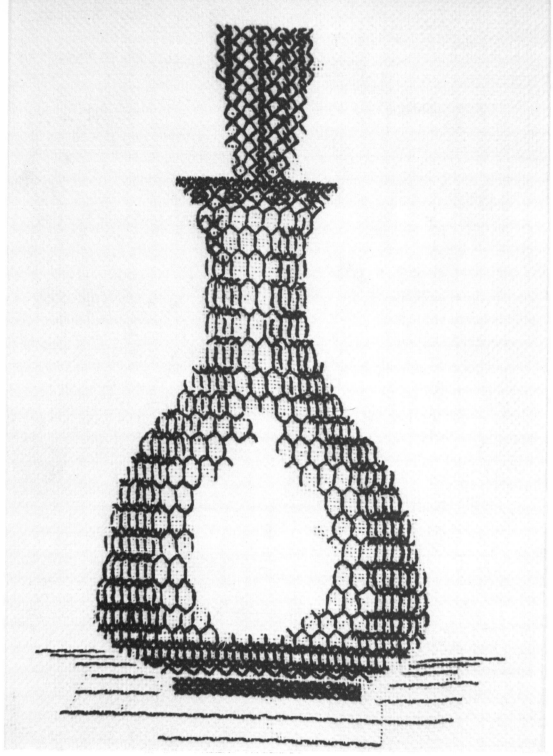

101 'The Decanter', by Diane Olive, 1983, Woking Adult Education Centre; tutor, Pamela Watts. 17.5 × 12.5 cm (7 × 5 in.). Linen, count 24/2.5 cm (1 in.). A single stitch pattern has been used to create a two-dimensional effect. The centre of the body of the decanter has been left unembroidered to get the lightest tone. The darkest tone at the edges is made by compressing the hexagon pattern and adding extra threads. This is what our eyes would see if the decanter were covered all over by a stretched net. Another pattern is used for the stopper, suggesting the facets of cut glass.

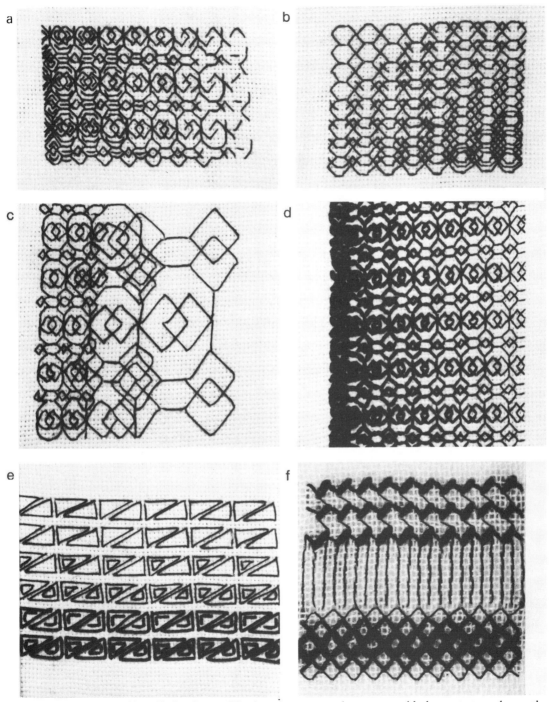

102 Six stitch samplers, (a) to (f) showing modification of blackwork patterns to give specific effects. (a), (b) and (c) all use only one thickness of thread. In (a) different stitches of the diaper pattern have been omitted, more on the right than on the left. In (b) the omissions are done in a more regular manner, with the greatest number on the left. In (c) the pattern is enlarged over successively more threads. In (d) and (e) the pattern is darkened by thickening the threads. (f) is the pattern that grew – a doodle on the fabric using three thicknesses of thread.

103 'Leaf', by Sybil Sims, 1983, Woking Adult Education Centre; tutor, Pamela Watts. 15 × 13.5 cm (6 × 5¼ in.), on linen, count 20/2.5 cm (1 in.). Each leaflet has a different diaper pattern which is graded by the thickness of the threads used. In one pattern on the left-hand side a line has been intentionally omitted around the cross stitches to lighten the tone.

104 'Kissimul Castle', by Margaret Humphrey, Surrey, 1982. 30 × 20 cm (12 × 8 in.), on pale grey linen, count 24/2.5 cm (1 in.). Two layers of fine black hexagonal net were applied for mountains; a thick, black, close pattern was used for the foreground shapes. Square stitch was randomized for the stones of the castle. Sewing cotton, shaded from white to black, was used to depict water; also used are no. 40 crochet cotton and various silk threads.

that many textures, both natural and man-made, were not equally dense over the whole area. The embroidery of Kissimul Castle (fig. 104) shows this variation in the stones of the building. There are many other examples of this technique throughout the book and attention is drawn to it in the captions.

To achieve this variation in stitching, the three methods just described are not suitable because they are too systematic, and may produce other different and unwanted prominent patterns, which could be distracting. Instead, the effect is achieved by leaving out, and/or adding, a stitch here and there. It can also be done by changing the thread in the needle to a different thickness when it runs out; this is a more random way than changing the thread at the beginning of a new line. A repeating regular pattern is the basis of blackwork, but here we need to lose some of its exact repetition. This does not come easily to most of us. One of my students overcame her difficulty by embroidering her pattern regularly, in the finest thread possible, over the whole area, thus making an even net of stitches. She then added thicker threads in the required places.

As an exercise in random variation I suggest that you work on your sampler the outline of a leaf or other interesting shape, not less than 5 cm (2 in.) across, using small tacking stitches in black sewing cotton. Choose a simple diaper pattern and vary it as I have suggested. Each time the thread runs out, use a different thickness in your needle. At least three different thicknesses of thread are necessary.

You must remember when using random varia-

105   Use one hand each side of the fabric.

tion in your work not to get carried away and forget the overall tone value that you previously decided upon.

There are embroidery cottons on the market known as random or shaded threads. The black ones vary from full black through shades of grey to white, repeating along the length. Short lengths of this can be cut and used to help you achieve variation. This has been used to depict the water in the distance in 'Kissimul Castle' (fig. 104).

General tips on working

Blackwork is close, exact work, so make it easy for yourself by choosing, as far as possible, a suitable environment. You will be able to work longer and

get better results. Bear in mind the following points:

1 Sit with your back to a good light. If you are right-handed, try to have the light coming over your left shoulder, and vice versa.

2 Sit on a comfortable chair of the right height.

3 Clamp your frame, if using one, in some way, or rest it at the correct angle on the table propped on some heavy books or a weighty object.

4 Try to have a plain area behind the frame. Too much detail in the background can be distracting. Try different materials on the table or behind your frame; some will show up the weave of the fabric better than others.

5 Do not try to carry on for too long; short breaks are necessary. An added bonus is that when leaving

or coming back to the work you can often see faults and ways out of difficulties, which were not apparent when you had your nose glued to the fabric.

6 Choose a small piece of work to begin with, using a fabric coarse enough to see easily. Blackwork is not a quick technique, and you may be discouraged if you are too ambitious at the start.

7 Use a short length of thread. A very experienced embroiderer suggests that the thread should not be longer than the length from the top of your little finger to your elbow. Most beginners take too long a thread in the mistaken belief that it will be economical. A short length allows the correct pull to be made in one movement and prevents tangling. Also, if it is too long the last bit of thread will become worn and fuzzy and lose its crisp look. A thread may become twisted; if it does, let the needle hang and the thread will untwist of its own accord.

8 Put one hand each side of the fabric; generally, the more able hand should be at the back. This hand has the more difficult job to do of finding the correct hole through which to bring up the needle.

Remember: the needle always goes in the *hole* between the threads of the fabric. Never *split* threads. Work with stabbing movements from the front to the back and vice versa; in other words, the needle is kept at right-angles to the fabric.

9 Start with a knot at the end of the thread. Pass the needle vertically down between the threads from front to back of the fabric, and about 1.5 to 2.5 cm ($\frac{1}{2}$ to 1 in.) from where you want your first stitch. Thus the knot will be lying on the top surface of the fabric. Later the knot will be cut off. It is best if the knot is placed so that the short length of thread to the first stitch on the back of the fabric is worked over by the pattern, so that it is secured. When you wish to change to another thickness of thread or it is too short to use, bring your needle up from the back of the work, through a hole, a short distance away from your last stitch, and leave the end loose on the surface of the fabric. Further stitches with a new thread will be worked over the length of thread at the back and it will be secured. Later cut off the end on the surface.

If any of these threads are not secure when the work is finished, you can thread the short end of thread under the stitches at the back of the fabric, using a small crochet hook or needle-threader if it is too short to thread in a needle. Do this firmly and beware of it showing on the front. Special care must be taken when starting and finishing a thread if the finished piece is to be laundered or dry-cleaned.

6. Making a panel

Now that you know something about stitch patterns and what you can do with them, you are ready, dare I say itching, to start a larger piece of work. For the sake of simplicity, I shall assume that this will be a rectangular or square panel.

Making a tone diagram

At this stage you will have made your design together with either a drawing or a paper collage showing tonal areas inside a rectangular frame (Chapter 3). From this you will need to construct a tone diagram. Trace the outlines of the design, its tonal areas and its frame on to a piece of tracing paper. Greaseproof paper is quite suitable. Ink in the outlines boldly and label each tonal area – dark, medium-dark, light etc. It is useful to mount this tone diagram on a piece of card which you can keep near the embroidery frame when working. It will be easier to handle than a piece of paper and will last longer. You will most likely need more than one copy of the tone diagram. You should always trace from the tone diagram directly, not from copies of it, since every time you trace there will inevitably be small inaccuracies.

Now you must decide the final size of your embroidery. The tone diagram may be the correct size, but if not, you will need to scale it suitably. In most cases this will mean enlarging. If you need to reduce the scale, the same procedure will apply, but you must interpret the following directions for a smaller rectangle instead of a larger one. Remember that if the lengths of the sides are doubled the area of the design, and consequently the work involved in embroidering, will be four times as great. Often a linear enlargement of one and a half times is sufficient.

Scaling

To make the enlargement in the same proportion as the design, make a tracing of the design and transfer it to the top left-hand corner of a large sheet of paper. Draw in the diagonal, from top left to bottom right-hand corners of the transferred design, and extend it downwards from the bottom right-hand corner. Measure the length of the diagonal, and then measure off from the bottom right-hand corner a length equal to this, multiplied by the amount you wish to enlarge your design. Thus, if the first diagonal is 16 cm ($6\frac{1}{2}$ in.) long and you wish to enlarge your design one and a half times, you will need to measure off a length of 24 cm ($9\frac{3}{4}$ in.) along the extended diagonal, starting from the bottom right-hand corner. This will be the diagonal of your enlarged design. Draw in the larger rectangle as shown in fig. 106. This will be the size of your embroidery, and it will have the same proportions as your original design. Now cut out the two rectangles. To ease the task of scaling, these must be divided up into smaller areas, and the easiest way to do this is by folding each in half and in half again to make four, and repeating to make 16 rectangular areas. Smooth out the two rectangles and ink in the fold lines.

In each of the 16 rectangular areas draw the outlines from the corresponding area of the smaller rectangle. If you find this difficult, then look for special landmarks in each area, such as the place where a line of the design cuts a grid line, and check by eye that you draw them in the correct positions. When you are satisfied that your scale diagram is absolutely correct, ink in the outlines. Keep your enlargement as simple as possible; too many lines can be confusing.

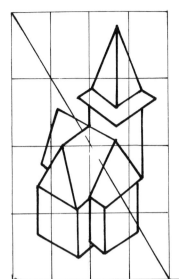

106 Scaling. The diagonal common to both rectangles ensures that both rectangles have the same proportions. If the proportions are altered and the resulting larger rectangle is divided as before, you will get a taller or a shorter design, according to which dimension you increase. This can be done intentionally to get various exaggerated effects.

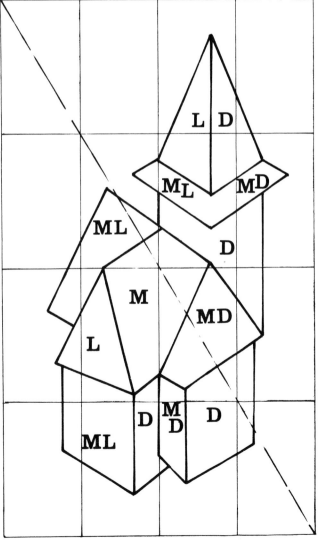

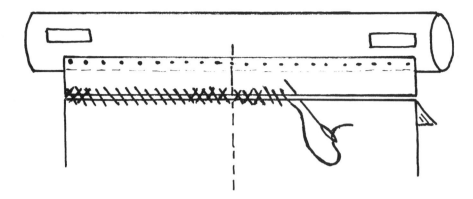

107   Sewing fabric to the webbing of a slate frame.

Choose either a slate frame or a canvas stretcher. As I stated previously, tambour frames can mark the fabric permanently.

Dressing a slate frame

Look at your design on paper and measure its length and breadth. Add at *least* 8 cm (3 in.) to each of these measurements to give a *minimum* border of 4 cm (1½ in.) around the design. It is a false economy to cut the fabric with an insufficient margin around the design. It can be extremely disappointing to find after hours of patient work that the final piece cannot be presented as you would wish. Before you put scissors to the fabric, make certain that you have two edges which are true to warp and weft respectively. A selvedge will be true to the warp. If necessary, pull a thread to find the weft. Now you can mark out your measurements on the material and use your scissors. Overcast the edge or machine a zigzag all round to prevent fraying.

If the fabric has a loose weave, it is advisable to sew on firmly a border of cambric or old sheeting all round. This will distribute the tension on the frame more evenly. Using a border in this way will be essential if your piece is small.

Now you are ready to attach the fabric to the frame. First separate the rollers from the stretchers. Mark the mid-points of the webbings indelibly. Turn over 1.5 cm (½ in.) of fabric on each of two opposite sides of your rectangular piece of material. The length of these two sides must not be longer than the length of the webbings. Mark with a pin the mid-point of each. Place the material, face side

down, with one of the marked sides along the free edge of one webbing. Pin the mid-point of the fabric to the mid-point of the webbing. Using strong thread, such as carpet thread, oversew the edges together, starting from the middle and working towards one edge of the fabric. Then go back to the middle and oversew the other half as shown in fig. 107.

Be sure to fasten off very securely. Attach the other marked edge of the fabric to the other webbing in exactly the same way. Now attach the rollers to the stretchers. If the length of the fabric is longer than can be tightened with the stretchers available, then you must roll the fabric around the rollers. Tension the fabric between the rollers and fix by the method provided – pins, pegs, screws, etc.

The free edges of the fabric must now be laced to the stretchers. This is done with string; the sort used by butchers for trussing is ideal. You will require a long, continuous lacing without knots, so I suggest that you buy a ball of such string. Do not cut off a length, but using a carpet needle or a large chenille needle, bring the end of the string up through the fabric about 1.5 cm (½ in.) from the edge, and close to a roller. Pass the end around the stretcher and back *up* through the edge of the material again, about 2.5 cm (1 in.) from the first stitch. Repeat regularly all along the edge of the material until you reach the other roller. Tie the end of the string tightly around the stretcher. Now, working back from this point, take the slack out of the lacing, but do not tighten as this will distort the edge of the fabric. When you have got back to the start of the lacing, cut the string and tie the end temporarily around the stretcher. Repeat the operation on the other edge of the fabric. Then tighten the lacing a little at a time on alternate sides until

108 Transferring a design to framed fabric, using tissue paper.

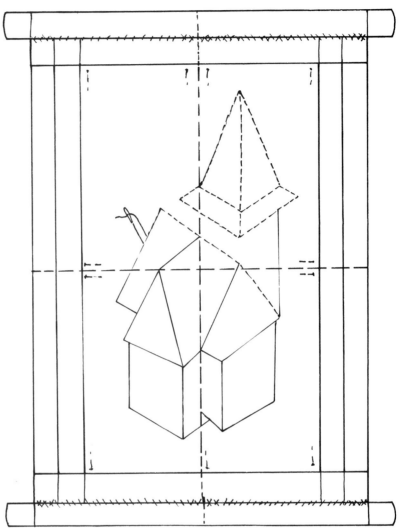

the fabric is pulled taut and square. Check carefully that the warp and weft threads are straight.

You will find, particularly with linen, that the tension in the fabric changes with the weather, so that slight adjustments may be necessary as the work progresses. For a diagram of a dressed slate frame, see fig. 93.

Dressing a canvas stretcher

Artists nail the canvas to the frame and then stretch it by inserting small wedges in the corners. For embroidery I prefer to make up a frame, and staple strong cardboard across the corners to keep a true rectangle. I then staple the fabric to the frame, pulling it evenly in both directions. Stretchers can be rather rough, particularly when staples have been removed from them, and should be smoothed with fine glasspaper. A heavy-duty stapler is a very useful tool, but drawing pins (thumb tacks) can be used instead. (See also fig. 94.)

Transferring the design to the fabric

There are many ways of doing this (see *Mary Thomas's Embroidery Book*), but for blackwork I recommend the following method. I always transfer the design with the fabric already stretched on the frame, as I find it easier.

109 'Building in Venice', by Joan Scott, Surrey. Varied
threads on coarse linen, count 20/2.5 cm (1 in.); 18 cm
(7 in.) square. There is a narrow black and gold frame
with no inner mount (not shown). A close pattern is used
on the left of the main building to contrast with the
lighter area on the right. The reflections are made using
one patttern, only faintly suggested in some areas.

1 On the full-size tone diagram, mark the mid-points of each side of the rectangular frame around your design, and join them to denote the horizontal and vertical lines. These must be parallel to the threads of the fabric when the design is transferred. If you have scaled your design as I have described, these lines will already be on your drawing.

2 Trace the design on to tissue paper, including the rectangular frame and the horizontal and vertical middle lines. I find a ball-point pen very useful for this.

3 Mark on the framed fabric the mid-points of each side and join with a tacking stitch in black sewing cotton. Be careful to follow one thread of warp and weft respectively, so that the design is transferred true to the weave of the fabric.

4 Matching up the mid-points, pin the tissue paper with your design to the fabric (see fig. 108).

5 With a small running stitch, tack around the outlines of the design using black sewing thread, and fasten off the ends securely. These tackings will have to be removed when you have completed the work. Sometimes it is difficult to remove the last traces of the running thread, and if a coloured thread is used it may be very conspicuous.

6 Carefully tear away the tissue paper, leaving the tacking stitches on the fabric. If you score the tissue paper with a sharp needle between the stitches, the paper tears more easily.

The advantage of this method is that the design can be altered during the embroidery by unpicking the tacking and replacing it in a different place, without leaving marks on the fabric.

You are now ready to start embroidering on the framed fabric with the design tacked on it.

Filling the tonal areas

Refer to your tone diagram on the card, which can be attached in some way to your frame or kept on a table close at hand.

Ideally, choose a large- or medium-sized area with a medium tone on which to start stitching. Sometimes it is best to start on the area which you find most interesting and about which you are most confident.

If you postpone what you think are the most difficult areas in a piece of work, the difficulty will sometimes solve itself. Never start an unfamiliar diaper pattern direct on to the final piece. Keep a small frame with a spare piece of the fabric on it to try out your patterns.

From the illustrated examples, you can see that a stitch diagram does not always indicate how the stitch will appear on the fabric. Also, the same stitch can look entirely different on a different fabric and/or in a different thread.

Choose a suitable pattern for the shape of the area. If you look at the cubes in fig. 111, you will see that Margaret Humphrey has chosen diaper patterns which are related to the area shapes. If she had put a square diaper pattern in one of the triangular shapes you would have been more aware of the pattern, and the effect would have been spoilt the design. This is an extreme example, but the diaper pattern should not quarrel with the shape of the area. Of course, if you want a certain effect, such as stripes, then you should use a pattern that gives you this effect.

Do not forget the lessons that you learned on your sampler; remember to get the tone value right and to use a random pattern if necessary. Start within an area where you have space ahead of you to develop your pattern, and preferably not at one edge. You need to get into the rhythm of stitching, with not too many stops and starts.

Small areas, particularly those with thin, narrow points, need experience and sometimes just a few stitches barely indicating the diaper pattern will suffice. The most suitable diaper patterns are those which relate to the size of the shape to be filled, and they vary from panel to panel.

If I could explain every point in detail, all originality would disappear. Each of the embroiderers whose work is illustrated has a style of her own. They are all different! In all of the pieces shown in this book, the best effects are those in which you are not immediately conscious of the pattern used. You should aim at the over-all effect. If the effect seems wrong, do not immediately unpick the whole area; sometimes a few stitches added here and there will make a great difference. When you come to the edge of the area to be filled, stop the diaper pattern at the tacked line. Sometimes you are faced with the dilemma of whether to go over or not quite up to the line. In most cases it is best to go slightly over it. When you look at the area after it has been filled, you can add or even take out a few stitches to correct it.

Do not use too many patterns on one piece of

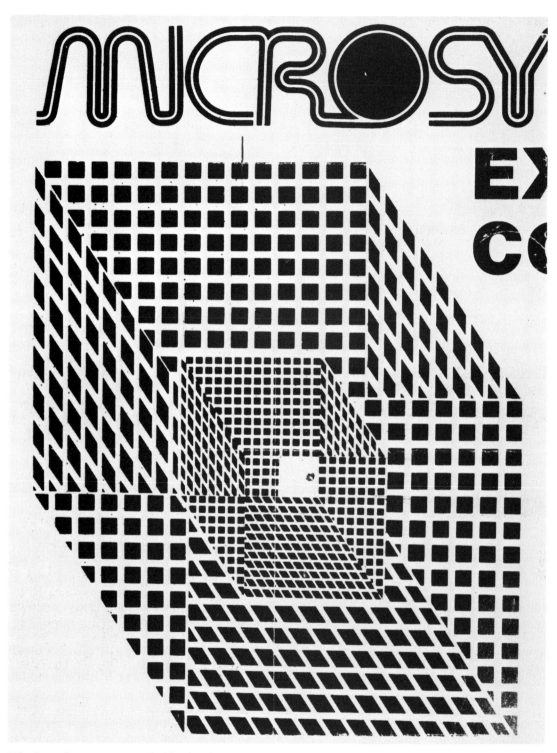

110   Logo for a computer trade-fair advertisement.

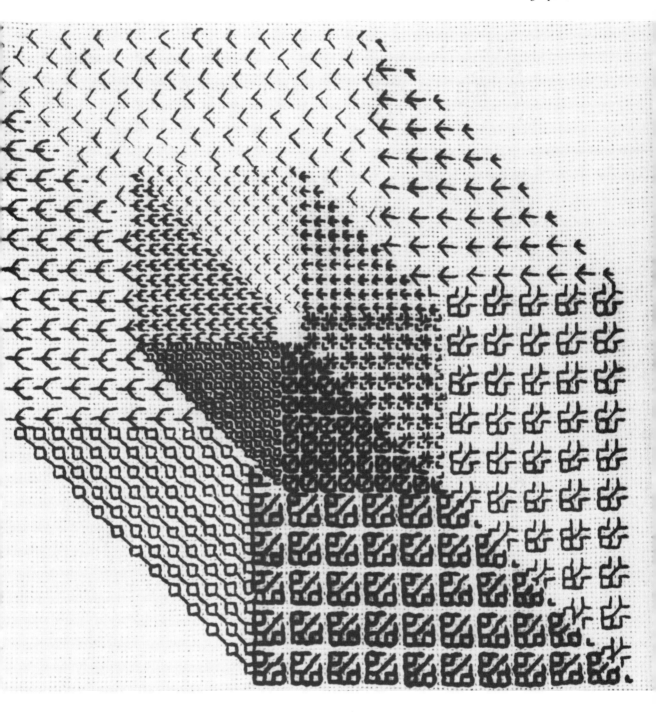

111 Embroidery based on the logo in fig. 110. 14 cm (5½ in.) square; fabric, off-white linen; count 28/2.5 cm (1 in.). The patterns in the outer cube are repeated in thicker threads and closer together in the inner cube, thus making the inner cube darker and more intense than the outer. This required much planning and fitting in of the patterns in the simple rectangular and triangular shapes. This piece is included in the *Blackwork Study Folio*, 1984, of the Embroiderers' Guild, and was embroidered by Margaret Humphrey.

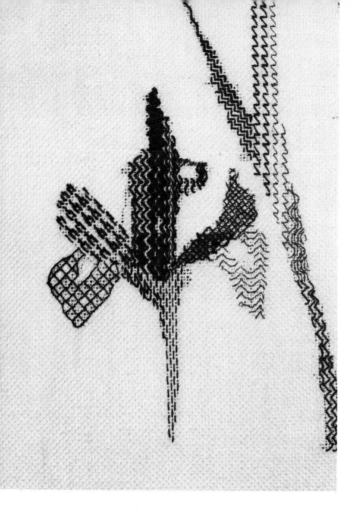

112 Detail from 'Irises', 1984, by Brenda Weekes, West Hampshire and Dorset Branch of the Embroiderers' Guild. Linen, off-white, count 22/2.5 cm (1 in.); 23 × 25 cm (9 × 13 in.); varied threads. This is a difficult subject because of narrow areas. The hanging petal on the right of the flower is in a very suitable stitch.

work. It is often better to use variations of the same diaper pattern. So many of them are related and work well together. Speaking for myself, I feel that some students use far too many different patterns in one panel, thus turning it into a sampler, not an artistic piece of work. First, make yourself a sampler with as many patterns as you wish and have time for; then use only a minimum of patterns in one panel, and vary their intensities. I think the possibility of achieving a good effect with a few stitches is a large part of my interest in blackwork. Remember to use the background to highlight the areas of stitchery. You did not carefully choose an expensive material in order to cover it all up.

Difficulties

If you find that at some stage of the embroidery you have lost your way and cannot see what to do next, it may help to look at your original source of inspiration and see if you have brought out the points which first attracted you. Do not be afraid of unpicking, but try not to do this too often as the black thread sometimes leaves grey marks on the linen.

Leave the work propped up somewhere you often pass; looking at it as you go about the house may give you the answer. As I suggested about designing, ask your family and friends what they think. You do not have to take their advice, but it may give you fresh ideas. Leave it for a while: pressing on when dissatisfied can be disastrous.

Knowing when to stop, that is, deciding when the panel is finished, is difficult. In embroidery you can add extra stitches *ad infinitum*. Do not be in a hurry to do this; it is very easy to over-embroider. If possible, leave several days between finishing the embroidery and mounting it. It can be helpful to cut a rectangular hole in a large piece of paper or card and pin this to the embroidery, so that the frame and all the lacing and webbing are masked. You will then see the shapes made between the design and the edge of the paper, and the tone values will be more obvious. Adjustments can be made and the panel reconsidered.

113 'Penguins', by Joan Roberts, West Hampshire and Dorset Branch of the Embroiderers' Guild. Natural linen, count 28/2.5 cm (1 in.); 21.5 × 25.5 cm (8½ × 10 in.); varied threads and beads. This design shows good use of a minimum number of patterns.

7. Mounting and framing an embroidered panel

So many good pieces of embroidery are spoilt by bad mounting. If you can get practical instruction for this operation, do so. I cannot stress too strongly that the fabric must be mounted evenly and squarely.

The mounting board is a piece of hardboard or card on which the embroidery is stretched and strung. The mount is the card which surrounds the mounted embroidery and covers up the edges of the embroidered fabric. For a window mount, a hole is cut in this card to the required size to show the embroidery, and sometimes lines are drawn or painted around the hole. The mount is sometimes covered in fabric, and card can be bought which has a special finish, such as linen or silk. The cut edges of the mount may be bevelled and inner mounts added if you wish.

The traditional method of framing an embroidery was by mounting it on a firm background of wood or card, generally in a rectangular form, and then cutting a window mount which was placed over the fabric. The whole was then framed with a picture frame and glazed if needed.

Nowadays there are many more unusual methods, particularly for embroidery techniques where the stitching or padding make conventional framing and glazing difficult. A more intimate connection between the shape of the stitching and the frame, and even doing away with the frame altogether, have led to many innovations, such as carrying the stitching partly over the mount. This is not the place to describe them; modern books on other techniques show good examples.

Here I shall describe mounting on hardboard after stretching the embroidery, and making a window mount. The latter can be dispensed with if you feel that the final frame is sufficient.

Removing the embroidery from a slate frame

Having decided that the embroidery is finished, carefully unpick the tacking thread around the design. If you originally put in rectangular tacking, leave this, together with the central horizontal and vertical lines. Undo the lacing and unpick the oversewing attaching the fabric to the webbing. The embroidered fabric is now free from the frame. Lay it down on a clean, flat surface and before stretching, make sure that all the ends of thread on the back are secure and tucked away so that they do not show on the front through the holes.

If the work does not lie completely flat and is puckered in any way, it will need to be stretched. Blackwork does not need so much stretching as some other forms of embroidery but it can be beneficial and ensures that the weave of the fabric is exactly true.

Stretching an embroidery

Lay two or more layers of damp blotting paper or damp absorbent fabric such as towelling, curtain interlining or flannel, on a clean drawing board. Place the embroidery face up on this, and with drawing pins (thumb tacks) pin out the material, stretching it slightly. Make sure the warp and weft are at right-angles to each other and that the tacked rectangle is not pulled out of true. Be generous with your pins. Leave the stretched embroidery in a warm place for about 24 hours, until it is dry. Then take out the drawing pins. You will find that the work looks smoother and better.

The mounting board

While the embroidery is drying, prepare the mounting board. Hardboard is generally used for this. The size must be such that at least 2.5 cm (1 in.) of the embroidery fabric can be turned over the edges on all sides. Within this size you can make the board any dimensions you wish. If the hardboard is cut for you at a shop, make sure all the angles are right-angles and that the edges are smooth.

The hardboard needs to be covered with a thick material such as felt, curtain interlining, domette or a thin synthetic wadding. To attach the fabric to the board, use a little glue at the edges and cut so that the fabric is exactly the size of the board. If it is taken over the edges, the final effect will be lumpy. Mark discreetly on the fabric the centre points of all four sides.

Because most of the evenweave fabrics on which blackwork is embroidered are open enough to show anything placed behind them, you must be careful to choose the right colour for covering the mounting board. White is not always the best choice; cream or a light beige often make the weave of the background more easily seen and give an interesting effect. The material should not be too thick. Trim the edges of the embroidered fabric so that it is at least 2.5 cm (1 in.) bigger all round than the hardboard, that is, the sides of the material must be at least 5 cm (2 in.) longer than the sides of the board.

Matching the mid-points of the board to the mid-points of the embroidery, lay the embroidery face down on the table and put the board padded side down on it. Trim the corners of the fabric diagonally as shown in fig. 114 (not too close to the corner). Fold upwards and crease the fabric at each corner along the dotted line.

Turn the side edges of the fabric over the board, and with a few pins secure them temporarily to it. When the corners are turned in, they must be neat. The folded diagonal edges should lie alongside each other and can be sewn together later. If the fabric does not fray easily and is not too thick, this is not difficult. Sometimes just a touch of glue on the middle of the edge of the diagonal cut will prevent fraying.

If the fabric frays readily, it is better not to trim the corners diagonally but to pull each fabric corner across the corner of the board and tuck in each side neatly and smoothly, holding them with a few pins.

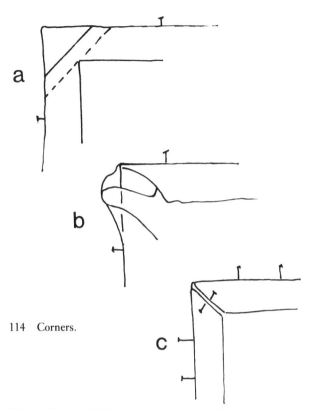

114   Corners.

If the fabric is thick, a certain amount of trimming can be done where there are more than two layers.

Using a continuous fine twine, string the embroidery over the board as shown in fig. 115, both horizontally and vertically with long stitches taken from side to opposite side and about 2.5 cm (1 in.) apart. A ball of twine is useful for this purpose, as no knots must impede the tightening process. Adjust the lacing in one direction by pulling the twine stitches individually until they are tight, before starting in the other direction. Do not pull too tightly. Keep checking that the work is still square on the board; so much embroidery is spoilt by crooked mounting.

Fasten off the twine in both directions, leaving a little for further adjustment; set the work aside for as long as possible. If, when you return to the work, you find it is not straight, you can adjust it slightly by loosening the twine, moving the board a little bit and retightening. Fabrics alter after being pulled and try to assume their original shape. When you are satisfied, fasten off the ends of the twine firmly. A piece of strong paper pasted over the back of the mounted embroidery gives a neat finish. A piece of fabric sewn over the back, or a thin card cover, can

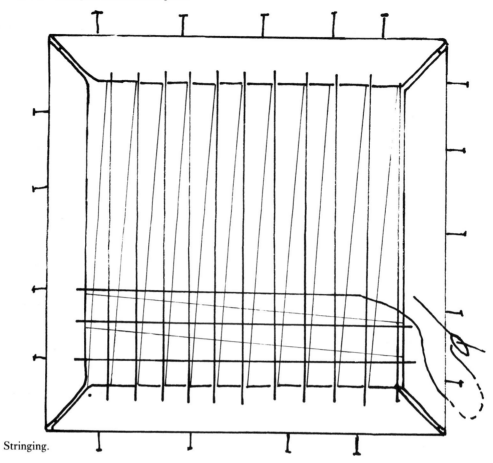

115 Stringing.

be used instead. All embroideries look better when mounted with the warp and weft of the fabric at right-angles to each other. Blackwork, because it is worked on the weave of the fabric, shows up any variation of this angle very clearly.

Another pair of hands is a great help in these methods of presentation and if you are doing them for the first time, try to get some help.

A very simple mount can be made by covering a piece of hardboard or thick card with a fabric such as hessian (wallpaper hessian is useful for this), and then sticking your mounted embroidery on to it. Because hardboard does not take hanging eyes easily, you must remember before covering the board to make holes, and put your string or wire through these for hanging the picture. The board will have to be significantly larger all round than the mounting board, but you can decide its proportions. If the covering material is thin, a layer of thick fabric should be put underneath it, as in mounting the embroidery. Again, watch the corners

for neatness. Fig. 128, 'Sydney Hobart 1975', was mounted in this way on a board covered with a deep-purple matt fabric. A painted, varnished or polished wooden board can be used instead.

Making and fixing a window mount

For a window mount, a hole is cut in a piece of mounting card. The whole card should be slightly larger than the hardboard you used under the embroidery.

The window can be rectangular, square, oval, circular or any other shape, but it must be absolutely in the centre horizontally – unless, of course, you mean it to be placed asymmetrically. It is usual to mount a picture with a slightly longer measurement below the window than above it. Your knives (a craft knife is best) must be very sharp and you must use a metal rule. The mount is then stuck on to the embroidery with a little glue all round the edge, or both pieces are put into a wood or metal frame and suitably sealed at the back.

Hanging eyes

If the eyes go into the hardboard and not into a separate frame, make sure that the screws do not penetrate as far as the embroidery fabric. They can cause rust marks, particularly in seaside districts. If you decide not to have a surrounding frame, it is sometimes better, as hardboard does not take screws easily, to make four holes in a horizontal line on the hardboard and thread fine picture wire through these, before putting the fabric on it, to make a hanger.

Glue and adhesive tapes

Do be careful when using glue. Never stick the embroidery to the mounting board. Use glue sparingly and well away from the embroidery area. After a long period the glue discolours and the fabric pulls and becomes puckered. A PVA adhesive is a suitable medium, but do not be too lavish with it.

Adhesive tapes are useful when mounting, but they may degenerate and lose their stickiness after a while. They may also darken, and leave unsightly marks. Double-sided adhesive tape is a great help, particularly in small pieces to hold something in place during mounting and framing.

Glazing (protecting with glass or plastic)

You may feel that it is necessary to protect your finished work by permanently covering it with a piece of glass or other transparent material. The use of glass when framing embroideries is a disputed matter. So often the reflections spoil the appearance of the embroidery. Non-reflecting glass can overcome this objection to a certain extent, but it often deadens the effect of the embroidery. Where padded or raised techniques are used, the glass must be well away from the surface. To my knowledge, many embroidered pictures without glass, hung in private houses for more than ten years, have not become dirty. Anti-static sprays have their uses in this respect. If you are embroidering for sale to art galleries, particularly those abroad, certain requirements are laid down regarding the durability of the mounting and framing materials, and glazing is generally demanded.

There are many ways of framing, and if you can afford to get a good professional to do the work for you, I recommend that you do so. These days more and more picture-framers understand the requirements of embroidery, and they have the tools, materials and expertise to enhance your embroidery by a good mount and frame.

The colour of the mount and frame

The colour of the mount and frame is, of course, a personal choice and depends on where the picture is to hang. Black surrounds are not always the best for blackwork; a subtle green or grey can show up the black embroidery better. I have seen a small black tree with a red (the colour of oriental lacquer) frame and it looked beautiful. One of my best results was a window mount covered with a sludgy green hessian.

The mount should add something to the picture but should not be too obvious. Some of the panels in this book are mounted as follows:

Fig. 31, 'Field at Compton', has white velvet around the embroidery and a narrow white metal frame. Using velvet presents problems and should be done with great care.

Fig. 28, 'Narrow Boat in Lock', has a black linen mount with an extra rectangular hole cut in it with the title of the embroidery showing through.

The back cover illustration, 'Activity', has a narrow strip of card, bound with embroidery threads in the colours of the embroidery, inside the cream card mount and a narrow gold frame.

There are such a variety of mounts and frames that I cannot deal with them all here, and there are good text books on the subject.

8. Clothing and other articles embroidered with blackwork

When making a garment to be embroidered with blackwork, choosing the fabric is the first consideration. It must be suitable for the embroidery (it must have a countable weave) and it must also be suitable for the particular garment. Some linens would answer the first requirement (countability) but because they crease very easily and do not always hang well, they would not be right for a skirt. A woollen or synthetic hopsack would be a better choice.

All garments must either be washable or suitable for dry cleaning. The threads used for the embroidery must be colour-fast and if it is to be an everyday garment, they will need to stand up to constant wear.

These requirements can be very restricting. In the blouse illustrated in fig. 116 Isabel del Strother has chosen a dressmaker's pattern which is suitable both for displaying the embroidery and for the fabric. It is fairly thick; a fine, thin material would probably have a high count and be difficult to embroider. Because many evenweave fabrics, particularly linens, fray easily, complicated dressmaking manoeuvres should be avoided. Keep it simple! This also applies to such items as embroidered boxes, book covers, lampshades, etc. With lampshades, the difficulty of hiding all your ends of threads must be overcome. A light behind an unmounted piece of work shows up all the otherwise hidden threads.

In designing the embroidery, the blackwork stitching should fill areas suited to the shape of the garment or object. Look at your pattern pieces. The shapes are very well thought out in the case of the waistcoat illustrated. Avoid stitch patterns that go over a large number of threads. Long stitches do not wear well. Borders are useful and easy to plan on a skirt, but on jackets and shirts they need adapting to go around armholes and necklines.

When embroidering pieces for a garment, do not cut out the pattern in the fabric first. Frame up a piece of the fabric and tack on it the shape of the pattern piece, allowing and marking at least as much as usual for turnings, and then embroider within the pattern area. The piece can then be cut out when all the embroidery has been finished. This means that more fabric may be required than for an unembroidered garment.

When planning ecclesiastical vestments there are traditional methods of construction, and colour and symbolism have to be considered. You should refer to standard works for these, but of course your design can be as modern as the clergy and congretion will agree upon. Just as in planning a religious or secular banner, the readability of the work from a distance must be a priority if it is to be seen by all. Church linen does not have to fulfil this function and can have fine, delicate designs embroidered on it.

Ordinary dressmaking and other appropriate techniques are used when making up the garment or object. Do not iron the actual embroidery more often than necessary.

116   Blouse embroidered by Isabel del Strother, 1976, on a white synthetic fabric, count 24/2.5 cm (1 in.), with black polyester buttonhole thread and some gold lurex stitches. Worn by Margaret Pascoe.

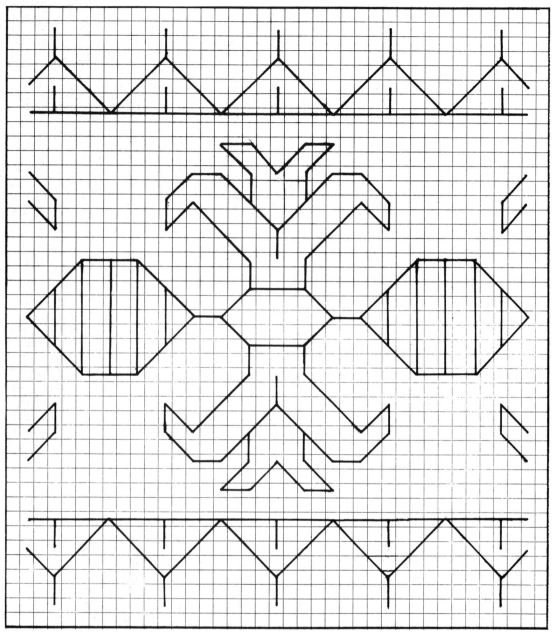

117 Stitch diagram of the pattern used in the blouse in fig. 116. Derived from a late sixteenth-century shirt in the Museum of Costume, Bath, England. The shirt also has a lace edging and gold braid.

118 Waistcoat embroidered by Marjorie Moore, Leicester, for her daughter. A woollen fabric was used and embroidered in varied black silks. The stitching is very dark at the bottom and light on the shoulders. The pattern was not based on anything in particular, but 'just grew'. The design follows the shape of the waistcoat. A flannel interlining was added to prevent the black stitching marking the lining and showing through. A border pattern can be seen at the centre front, but it becomes part of the whole embroidery at the bottom edge. The embroidery continues over most of the back of the waistcoat. Worn by Jennie Parry. (*Photograph by permission of Jennie Parry.*)

119 Box by Patricia Gaffer, Leicester; tutor, Wendy
Williams. This jewellery box is covered with natural
linen, count 28/2.5 cm (1 in.) The size is 11 cm (4½ in.)
square, and 6 cm (2¼ in.) high. The building depicted is
St Michael's Church, Ramsey, Essex. The embroidery is
in fine silks, and several patterns are used for the stones
and roof of the church, and others for the trees. Four
small motifs are embroidered on the sides of the box,
which are slightly padded, and the inside is lined with a
red moiré silk. For methods of constructing boxes, see
Embroidered Boxes and other Construction Techniques, by
Jane Lemon.

9. Mixed techniques and experimental work

Putting two or more embroidery techniques together in one piece of work used to be frowned upon by the purists, yet we have many examples of it in our textile museums. Some eighteenth-century waistcoats were embroidered in pulled work and then quilted. As I have said earlier, experiment and do what you wish in order to achieve the required effect.

Appliqué

Appliqué of opaque fabrics is often used rather than stitching to make the darkest tone. Black felt, velvet, suede, kid, plastics or corduroy can be applied with good effect and silks, satins and moirés give their own specific quality to the design. Applied fabrics generally need padding and will lie better over it, but each panel needs a separate decision.

Quilting, surface stitching and beads can be added over the appliqué (see fig. 120). Other fabrics that can be applied for a different effect are nets and other transparent materials. (See figs 59, 104, and 69). In these examples net has the same effect as a very fine, simple hexagon stitch pattern. Cotton net is softer and more subtle than nylon net, but more difficult to get. Millinery nets (veils) have larger holes and give a different effect. To hold the net in place, black invisible thread is useful; the stitch should go over only one thread of the net, and be very small. There are two kinds of so-called 'invisible' thread on the market, one black and the other white. They certainly show up less than cotton or silk threads, but are difficult to use because of their springy nature. This makes it imperative that the starting and the finishing of the thread be done with

extra care. Sometimes pulling a length of thread tightly between the first finger and thumb throughout its length, before using it for sewing, makes it easier to use. If you wish, you can work blackwork patterns over the net after it is applied, or on it before it is applied. The rules for net embroidery should be followed for this last suggestion, as explained in *Mary Thomas's Embroidery Book*.

Embroidering through the laid net is not easy; the coarser the net the better, and square nets are better than hexagonal ones. In many cases, the holes in the evenweave fabric are out of step with the holes in the applied net. Sometimes just a few lines of long straight stitches in black thread on the net will give the effect you need.

Painting or spraying the background

The introduction of the use of paint, ink and dyes has made a great impact on modern embroidery. I give examples of texts covering this field in the bibliography. Methods such as tie-dye and batik have long been used in fabric decoration and as backgrounds for various types of embroideries.

In spraying or painting fabrics, many forms of pigments can be used. Among these are aqueous solutions or suspensions such as water-colours and fabric dyes, aerosols such as household and motor-car paints, and specialized pens or pencils, which can be used with or without water. Pigments can also be sprayed from diffusers such as those used to spray fixatives on to charcoal or pastel drawings. Spatter work, that is, paints spattered on to masked fabric from a toothbrush, is another means of colouring before beginning the embroidery. A mask or stencil is essential in order to keep the pigment

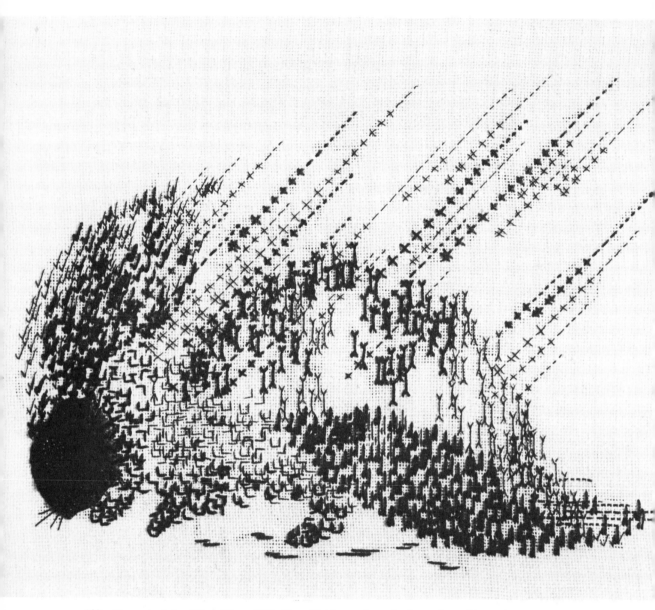

120 'Porcupine', by Olive West, 1973, New Malden Adult Education Centre; tutor, Margaret Pascoe. Unusual blackwork patterns give a sense of direction and there is good randomization of patterns. The nose is made from a piece of black kid padded with felt and applied to the linen. Black beads are stitched through kid and felt to give texture. (*Photographs by Valerie Campbell-Harding.*)

confined to the correct area for all these methods.

In blackwork, background painting and spraying is a way of emphasizing tonal values and thus saving time in intricate stitching. It is also a way of introducing colour. Examples are shown in figs 36, 122 and 123.

Padding and quilting

This is done by laying either felt or wadding under certain areas after embroidering and then quilting with a fine thread to enhance the design. General embroidery books such as *Mary Thomas's Embroidery Book* explain methods of quilting, and padding

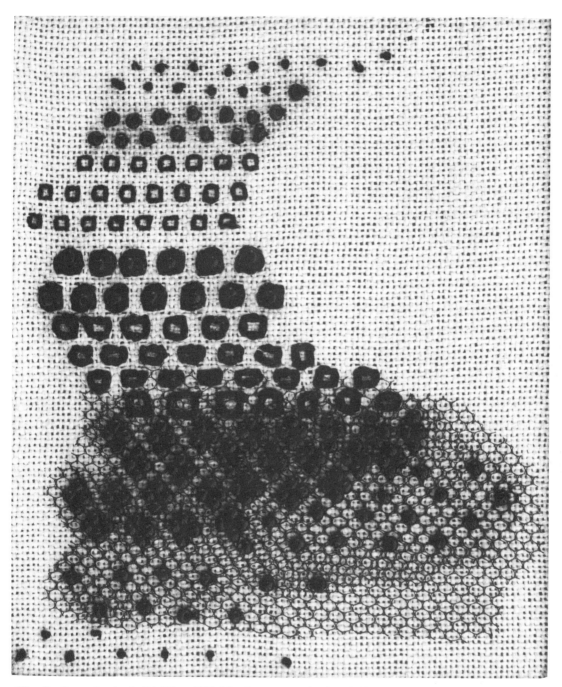

121 Small sampler, by Judith King, 1982, Manchester Polytechnic. It is an experimental piece; the blackwork patterns are very simple and the gradation from dark to light and small to large pattern is effective. Two layers of net, beads and thick threads are used. The curved edge of the overall shape gives movement to the design. This piece is now in the *Blackwork Study Folio*, 1984, of the Embroiderers' Guild.

122 'Face', by Betty Morris, 1983, Woking Adult Education Centre; tutor, Pamela Watts. Hardanger fabric, natural linen colour, count 22 holes/2.5 cm (1 in.). 15 × 12.5 cm, (6 × 4½ in.) A minimum of blackwork patterns is used. The fabric is painted on the left-hand side, depicting shadows. The angular, irregular shapes of the stitches in the lower part are reminiscent of jet beads. The contrast between the thick and thin threads is dramatic. The origin of the design was a newspaper portrait.

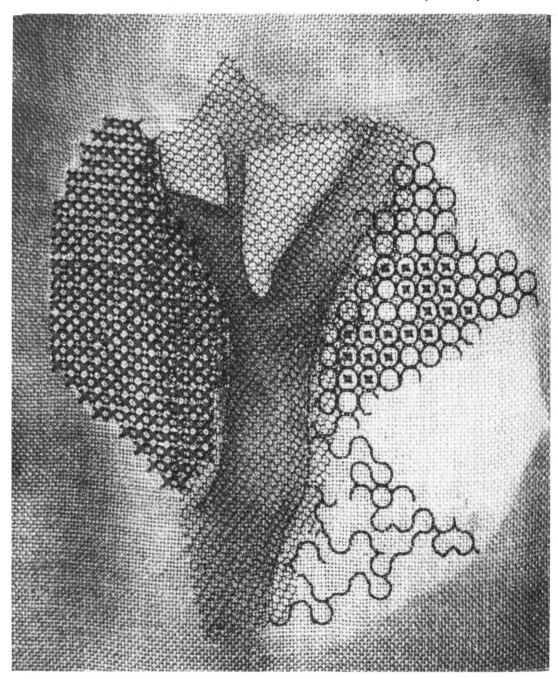

123 'X-ray of Shell', by Carolyn Stephens, 1984, Godalming Adult Education Centre; tutor, Vicky Lugg. Fine linen, 16×18 cm ($5\frac{1}{2} \times 6\frac{1}{4}$ in.). See fig. 78 for design shapes. After embroidering with black silk, the fabric was padded from behind and quilted with a back stitch around a sprayed area in the middle. Underneath the linen an iridescent lurex fabric glints through the holes. Black net is also applied and the blackwork patterns follow the shape of the holes in the net.

under appliqué is explained in *Metal Thread Embroidery* by Barbara Dawson.

Blackwork used as a background

In Assisi work, long-armed cross stitches are used to fill the background, and the motifs are left unembroidered. Blackwork diaper patterns can be used in the same way. It is important that the boundary between background and motif is definite, but an outline is not essential. Examples of this variation of blackwork are shown in figs 54 and 125.

In an article in *Embroidery*, 26 (1975), p. 83, Muriel Best describes how 'A Cube with a View' (fig. 126), was made. In this piece, very delicate blackwork was used to embroider the background of the clouds, and the main theme was worked in surface stitches.

124 'Balconies', by Gwen Holloway, 1984, London College of Fashion; tutor, Anthea Godfrey. Medium linen. The balcony rails are made of millinery wire and actually stand away from the fabric. Fine blackwork patterns depict the flowers and the building. Thick stitches emphasize the lower parts of the balconies.

125 'Chuffie', by Pat Rossington, 1984, Hampton School of Needlework; tutor, Betty Sankey. White linen, count 30/2.5 cm (1 in.); 49 × 39 cm (19½ × 15½ in.). This panel is unusual in that the background is embroidered much more than the dog. This was intentional, as West Highland terriers are white. The black nose was made by couching short loops of bouclé wool on to the linen.

126 'A Cube with a View', by Muriel Best, Surrey, 1975. 15 cm (6 in.) square. Surface stitchery with the background to the clouds interpreted in blackwork. Muriel Best, *Embroidery*, 26 (1975), p. 83. This piece is now in Oxford Museum. (*Photograph by permission of Valerie Campbell-Harding*.)

Pulled work is used in the Embroiderers' Guild transfer panel shown in fig. 129(a), and was often used in conjunction with blackwork for table linen in the 1930s. A sampler combining drawn thread and blackwork is shown in fig. 127.

Other techniques that you could combine with blackwork are canvas work and machine embroidery. It is easiest if the technique to be used with blackwork is also a counted-thread method, but this does not rule out experiments.

It would be difficult to combine blackwork with a technique that manipulates the fabric, such as smocking and tucking, because blackwork needs a flat surface. Smocking, like many other embroidery techniques, is passing through an experimental phase, and one could try smocking or pleating a piece of blackwork using black threads, to produce another pattern. Smocking is often used on striped, checked or otherwise patterned material to good

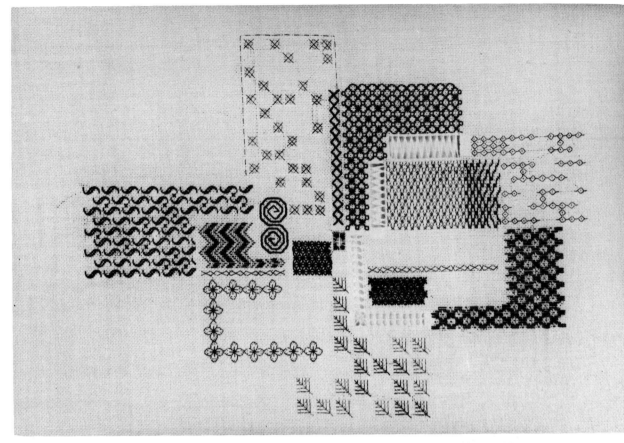

127 Sampler embroidered by Mary Thomson at the Royal School of Needlework, London; tutor, Moyra McNeill, 1970s. 37.5 × 27.5 cm (15 × 11 in.). Natural linen, count 22/2.5 cm (1 in.). This sampler shows a great variety of diaper patterns and threads; some drawn-thread work is included. Note the skilful use of very fine threads for light areas. The rise in the cost of linen is reflected in the size of this sampler. Most embroiderers today would use a piece about 15 cm (6 in.) square.

effect, but I cannot recollect seeing it used on a previously embroidered fabric. Also, it would be possible but not easy to insert a section of manipulated fabric in a piece of blackwork, and vice versa.

Coloured blackwork

The use of colour has been mentioned several times in previous chapters. Some embroiderers find dark stitches difficult to see and I have known some who said that such work is depressing. The blackwork diaper patterns can, of course, be worked on col-oured fabrics using coloured threads. The term blackwork applies more to the stitches and the technique used rather than to the colour of the threads.

Colour can be introduced in many ways:

1 A black or contrasting thread can be used on a coloured background. 'Chessboard for Joseph' (fig. 49) was embroidered using black threads on red linen with a little gold added. A light thread such as white, cream or a pastel colour can also be used on a dark fabric. Both of these examples are still, in essence, monochrome techniques.

2 Threads of one additional, strongly contrasting colour can be used with the main stitching. An example of this is the gold thread used in fig. 95, and in the motifs inspired by wrought-iron work in fig. 41, where red blackwork patterns and canvas-work stitches lie alongside black diaper patterns.

3 More than one colour of thread can be used in one piece of work. Daphne Nicholson has done this

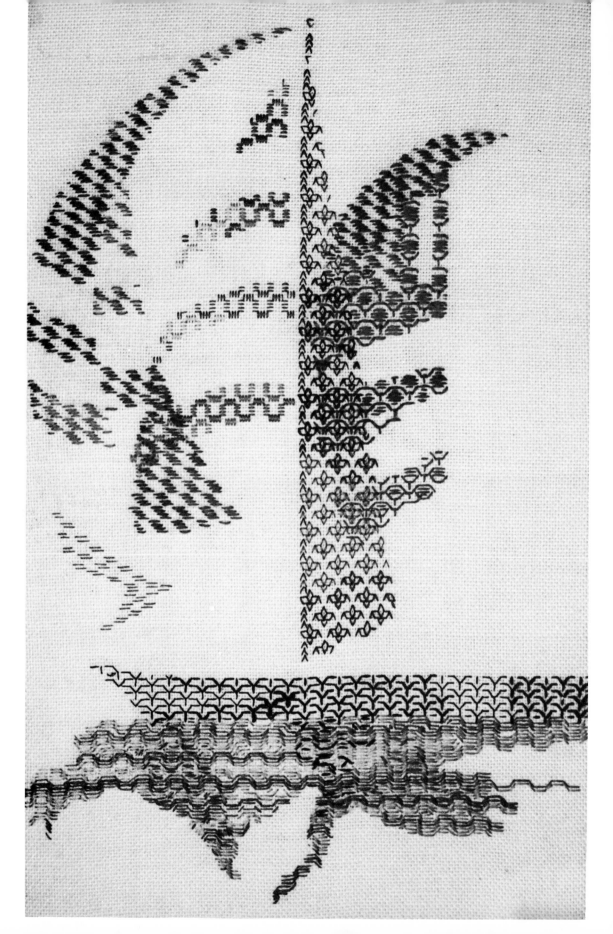

in 'Activity' (back cover), using a single colour for discrete areas.

Another variation mixes colours throughout the embroidery and the technique becomes fully polychromatic. This technique is used in 'Sydney Hobart 1975' (fig. 128). In all cases, the diaper patterns are still used to denote an area.

I was first attracted to this variety of blackwork after doing some exercises in overlapping patterns (see fig. 136). I thought that by mixing different-coloured stitches, new colours would emerge just as overlapping nets, chiffons and other transparent fabrics make new colours. I found that this did not always happen with coloured blackwork. Perhaps the fabric in between dilutes the colour too much. This could be overcome by using a colour-sprayed background. If another colour is sprayed on an adjoining area, allowing a little mixing where the two areas meet, a few stitches could be made in appropriately coloured threads over this intermediate zone with interesting effect.

If you like colour mixing and wish to test it in embroidery, a good exercise would be to stitch every horizontal stitch in a row of diaper patterns in one colour, every vertical stitch in another colour, and the diagonals in yet another colour. The result could be interesting.

I agree with the statement in the Embroiderers' Guild *Blackwork* leaflet (1984) that 'the multi-coloured threads alter the character of the method'. Perhaps part of the appeal of blackwork is in its precision, and in the fact that every stitch is equally important and completes a pattern. This is not so evident in polychromatic blackwork and it may not appeal to the same extent. Black and white used in embroidery have an elegant formality, just as they do in clothing. Nevertheless, coloured blackwork is a fascinating form of embroidery, and worth trying.

Remember that you have an extra dimension with which to experiment. If you decide to have an area a particular colour, let us say green, you can vary the colour of the green threads as well as their thickness. Thus, if you are using a crewel wool, such as Appleton's, you could embroider with many of the shades of green which are available, within the one area, keeping to the same diaper pattern. Also, as with black threads, do not forget to exploit the matt or shiny nature of the threads. The overall area will still be green.

There is a goldwork technique called *or nué* (Italian shading), in which gold threads are couched with coloured threads, and the gold is thus covered to a greater or lesser extent with colour. For the colour to have much effect it must be strong and vivid, unless a very subtle, subdued effect is wanted. I think that this also applies to polychromatic blackwork, especially where the stitches do not lie very close together. Thus some close darning stitches like the Florentine patterns used in figs 55 and 60 would be appropriate. Very fine coloured threads do not have the impact that black threads have.

In Chapter 5 I showed how tones can be made by varying the thickness of the thread and the closeness of the stitches. When using colour, do not forget that you have another variable. You can produce your tones by varying the shade.

When using black threads on a white ground one should theoretically be able to introduce intermediate tones by using grey threads. In *Needlework School*, Daphne Nicholson says: 'When using a range of black threads add a fine grey thread to extend the lightest tone.' In my experience, one is limited by the lack of shades of grey available commercially. Greys are all tinted by another colour such as blue or yellow, producing cold and warm greys respectively. In experiments to produce a graded series of grey tones as in fig. 53, dyeing my own threads using different dilutions of a black dye was not successful.

The mind boggles at the possible permutations and combinations within coloured blackwork, and the days are not long enough to try them all.

128 'Sydney Hobart 1975', by Margaret Pascoe, 1978. Synthetic hopsack; count 20/2.5 cm (1 in.); 48 × 28 cm (19 × 11 in.). Embroidered with wool and cotton threads in blues, greens, purples and pinks. There is some superimposition of diaper patterns on the sails, and the boat is embroidered in tree-stitch pattern in varied thicknesses of threads. The design was taken from a newspaper photograph. The sails are shown moving off the design area and the stern of the yacht is out of the picture on the right, thus emphasizing a sense of movement.

10. Some interesting stitch patterns

In 1955 the Embroiderers' Guild advertised for sale a transfer. This could be bought in two sizes priced one shilling and sixpence, and ten pence respectively, post free.

An unknown embroiderer worked this design on fine natural linen, count, 35 threads per 2.5 cm (1 in.) in blackwork patterns, and added a ring of pulled-fabric stitches. This piece, which I call 'The Bells' is now part of the *Blackwork Study Folio* (1984) of the Embroiderers' Guild. The transfer is no longer available.

In this embroidery, the diaper patterns are very delicate and are sewn in silk threads, probably Filoselle. Because of the fineness of the stitching and the not-too-heavy outlining in stem stitch, the work is not so static as are many other pieces of this period. The stems and tendrils, also in stem stitch, are curved, which helps the movement in the design.

Seven different diaper patterns are used, and stitch diagrams for six of them, numbered from the top in a clockwise direction, are illustrated in fig. 129(b). The stitch diagram for number 7, the windmill, is fig. 130. This stitch is used in a tray cloth embroidered by Osyth Wood (fig. 24), as also is stitch pattern number four from 'The Bells'. Perhaps Osyth Wood also embroidered 'The Bells'.

Mobile stitch patterns

Windmill stitch

The centre of the pattern is a cross made of five equal squares. The diagonal stitches, the sails of the windmill, which lead away from these squares give the pattern its mobility. They all meet in one point; this means that eight threads go into one hole of the fabric and therefore a thick embroidery thread is not practical. A suggested variation is embroidering the cross in a thicker thread than that used for the sails (see fig. 130).

Ravenna mosaic stitch

This was based on a drawing of a mosaic pavement at Ravenna, Italy. It has a rippling, two-dimensional effect which I have tried to enhance by adding small directional stitches on the fabric. The original drawing appeared in *Blackwork Embroidery* by Geddes and McNeill (see figs. 131, 132).

'Trees'

The use of thick and thin threads in lines and the angles between the lines give a ridged effect to the embroidery (see fig. 133).

Curved stitches

In fig. 134, diagonal stitches combine with the horizontal and vertical ones to make the patterns look curved.

Strapwork patterns

In fig. 135, the stitches are so arranged that they give the effect of plaiting as in basket work. This effect can also be seen in fig. 51.

129(a)   Guild transfer. W22 and W23.

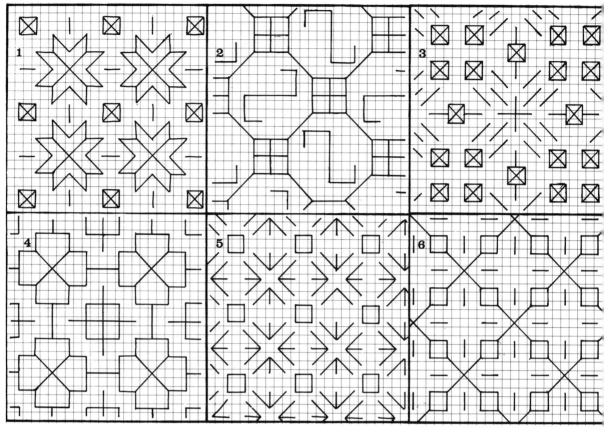

129(b) Six stitch diagrams from fig. 129(a), numbered clockwise from the top.

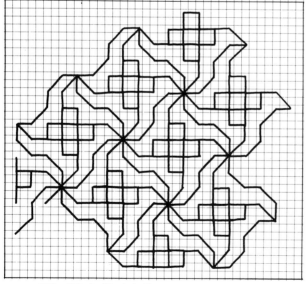

130 Windmill stitch diagram.

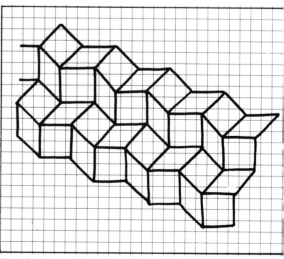

131 Ravenna mosaic stitch diagram.

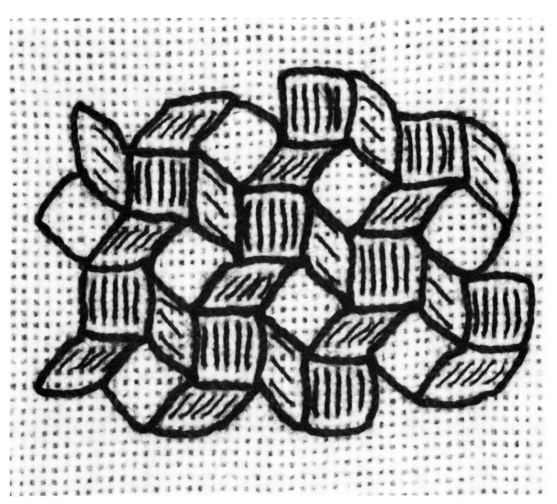

132   Ravenna mosaic stitch sampler.

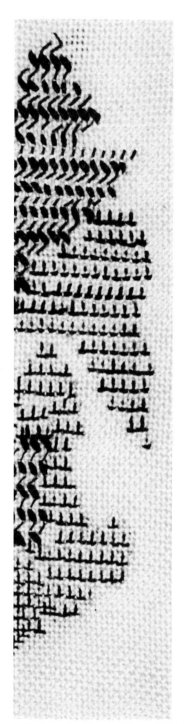

133 Detail of 'Trees', by Valerie Palmer, 1984, Woking Adult Education Centre; tutor, Pamela Watts. Embroidered on medium linen, with two thicknesses of black thread.

Overlapping a stitch pattern

If you embroider a simple stitch pattern openly in a medium thickness of thread, the same pattern can sometimes be repeated, starting it on the same line but one or two threads further along the line.

This can again be varied by using a different thread for the repeat, when an echo or a shadow-like effect is made. If the pattern is sufficiently open, another repeat can be made before you catch up with the second pattern. All sorts of new patterns can emerge by moving a pattern up or down, but it soon becomes complicated. This process can be used to good effect if you change the colour of the thread (see fig. 136).

Superimposed patterns

If you choose two very simple diaper patterns, these can be embroidered one on top of the other. This will not work with all patterns, and you must experiment on a sampler to find out what is possible. Again, varying the colour of the threads adds interest (see fig. 137).

Patterns in which the background predominates

Mrs Christie says in *Samplers and Stitches* (1929):

Working by the counted threads of the ground makes the stitches exactly alike and it brings in the fabric to help in the composition of the pattern and this is always in embroidery a pleasing treatment. In fact the more fabric and stitching can be interdependent the better the results. These geometrical treatments are as useful for the background as for the pattern.

In the examples of stitch patterns shown in figs 138 to 141, it is sometimes the stitchery that predominates and sometimes the warp and weft of the fabric, thus illustrating Mrs Christie's remarks.

Turning a corner for a border pattern

This is illustrated in fig. 142. Work out the pattern on squared paper and note how many threads are required for the width of the pattern. On another piece of squared paper, draw a corner of a border the same width and mark in the diagonal on the

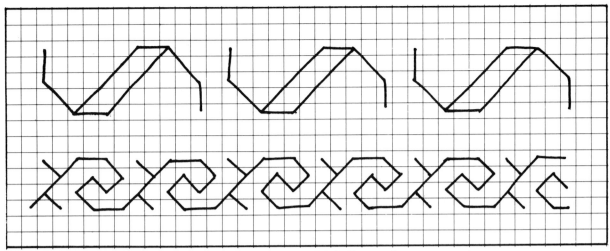

134 Stitch diagram for S stitch; see also fig. 127, and the border from Jane Seymour's cuff, fig. 30(b).

135 Stitch diagrams for two strapwork patterns.
(a) The border from 'Chessboard for Joseph', fig. 49.
(b) A stitch from a sampler, fig. 25.

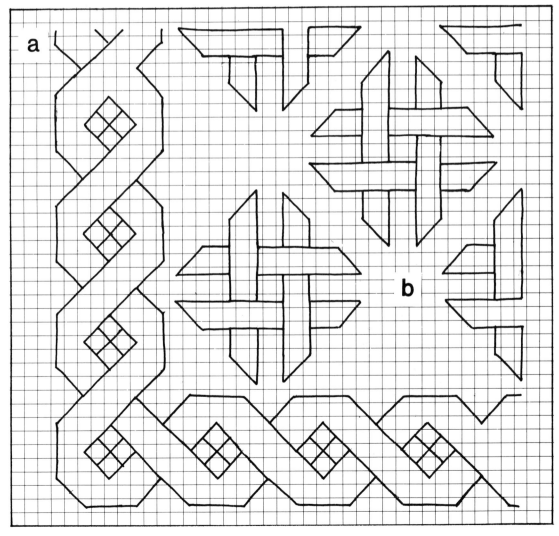

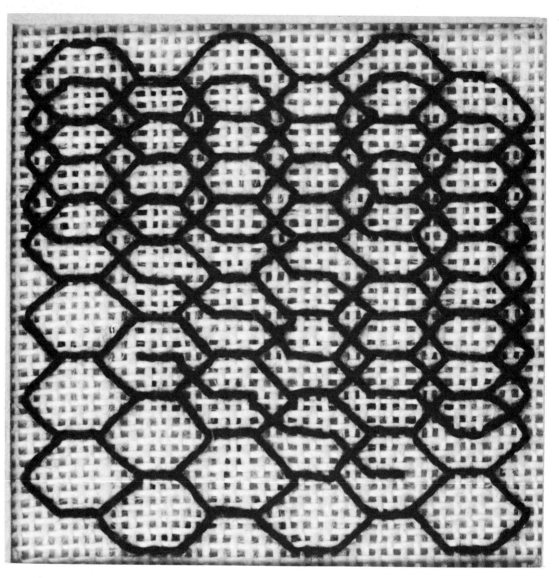

136 Overlapping a stitch pattern.   137 Sampler of superimposed patterns.

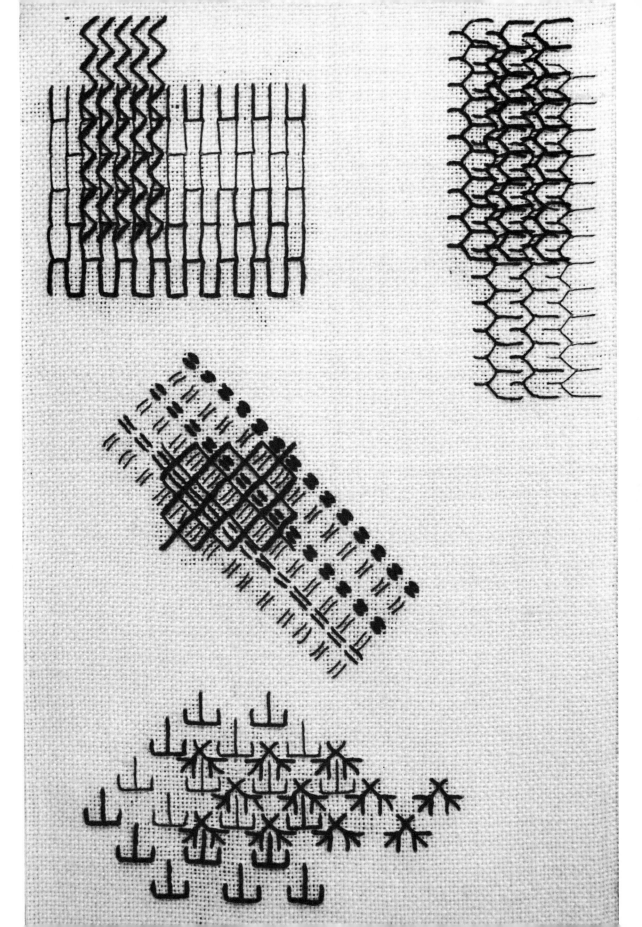

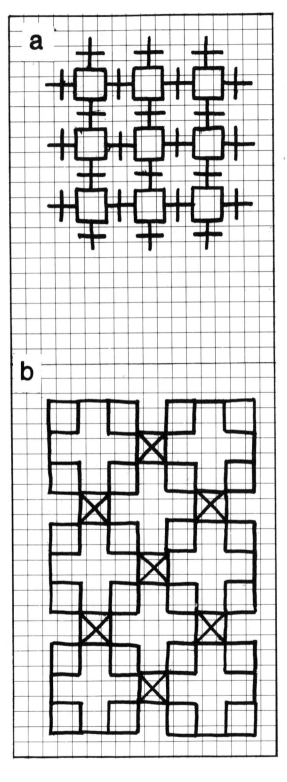

138 Stitch diagrams of two stitches from fig. 139 where the white pattern predominates.

139 (a) and (b) Details of two squares from 'Chessboard for Joseph'; in each case the background pattern is prominent. In (c) the dense blackwork patterns accentuate the central warp and weft threads, making a secondary lattice. The effect is achieved by the regularity of the stitches.

a

b

c

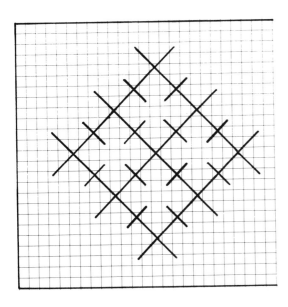

140   Stitch diagram for fig. 141(b).

141(a)   Fifteenth-century wrought-iron grating.
(b) Sampler of a simple diaper pattern to show the interdependence of fabric and thread. Three thicknesses of black silk are used. With the thickest threads the white crosses of the background create the pattern. With the thinnest thread one sees two patterns, the black network and the white crosses. This is a copy of a stitch pattern by Elizabeth Geddes, 1955.

a

b

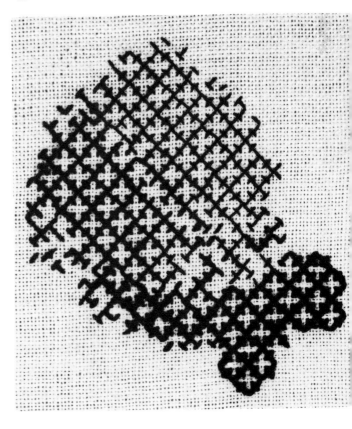

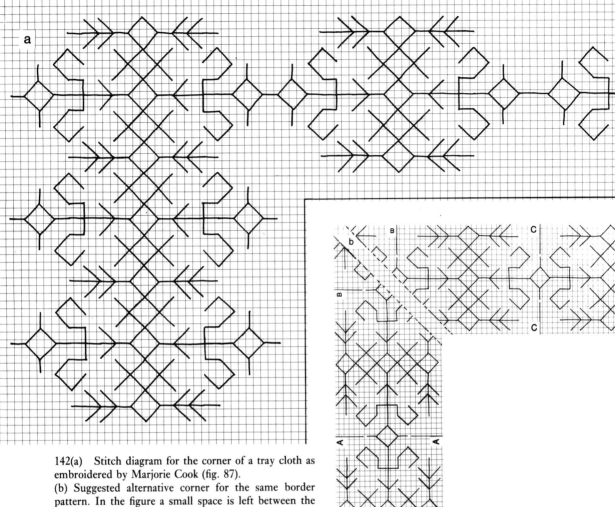

142(a) Stitch diagram for the corner of a tray cloth as embroidered by Marjorie Cook (fig. 87).

(b) Suggested alternative corner for the same border pattern. In the figure a small space is left between the diagonals to make the construction more obvious. The dotted lines would be together and not seen on the actual embroidery.

corner (the dotted line in the figure). Mark on the first piece of squared paper the places where the pattern repeats (dotted lines A and B in the figure).

Pencil in the stitches from A to B on one side of the second piece of paper, leaving out all the stitches past the diagonal line on the empty side. Turn the paper around and pencil in stitches from line C to B, ending again at the diagonal. You will find that on the corner your stitches will meet up to make a new pattern. Any gaps may be filled in to make the pattern look continuous. If you place a small mirror on the diagonal after pencilling in one side of the border, you can see in the mirror what will happen on the other side.

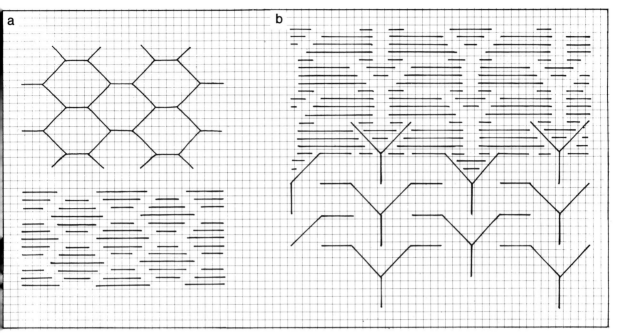

143 Negative and positive stitch patterns.
(a) Positive and negative hexagon patterns. These are out of step vertically, but in step horizontally.

(b) Positive and negative tree patterns merging into one another. In one motif of fig. 41 the background has a black/white negative tree pattern.

Positive and negative stitch patterns

If you look at any simple stitch pattern, a hexagon for example, you can see that the spaces between the threads could be filled in with short parallel stitches. These darning stitches make a pattern which is the negative of the first. In a piece of work the positive and negative patterns work well next to each other, one being an echo of the other. It is not practical to do this variation for all diaper patterns.

Further variation could be made by using different threads. If you find it difficult to work out the negative pattern, put in the positive stitches first (in pencil on squared paper or fine thread on the fabric), and embroider straight stitches in the spaces between. Then remove (rub out or unpick) the positive stitches.

137

Book List

Benn, Elizabeth (ed.), *Blackwork*, The Embroiderers' Guild, Apartment 41, Hampton Court Palace, East Molesey, Surrey, 1984

Brown, Pauline, *Embroidery Backgrounds: Painting and Dyeing Techniques*, Batsford, London, 1984

Christie, Mrs Archibald, *Samplers & Stitches*, Batsford, London, 1929; revised 1950; reprinted 1985

Coats Sewing Group, *Modern Spanish Blackwork*, Anchor Embroidery Book no. 755, J. & P. Coats Ltd, Paisley, Scotland

Cope, Anne & Jane, *Picture Framing*, Pan, London, 1981

Cornelius, Rosemary, Doffek, Peg, & Hardy, Sue, *Exploring Blackwork*, The Sinbad Series no. 1, Box 273, Ellington, Conn. 06029, USA, 1974

Dawson, Barbara, *Metal Thread Embroidery*, Batsford, London, 1968; reprinted 1986

Denne, de, Lynette, 'Thoughts on Blackwork', *Embroidery*, 24, 1973, pp. 84–6

Drysdale, Rosemary, *The Art of Blackwork Embroidery*, Mills & Boon, London, 1975

Dye, Daniel Sheets, *Chinese Lattice Designs*, Dover Publications, New York, 1974

East, Mary G., 'No-waste paper cuts', *Embroidery*, 19, 1968, pp. 14–15

Edwards, Joan, *Small Books on the History of Embroidery: Black Work*, Bayford Books, Dorking, England, 1980

Embroiderers' Guild Practical Study Group, *Needlework School*, Windward, London, 1984, pp. 154–9

An Encyclopaedia of Ironwork, Ernest Benn Ltd, London, 1927

Geddes, Elizabeth, & McNeill, Moyra, *Blackwork Embroidery*, Mills & Boon, London, 1965; reprint, Dover Publications, New York, 1976

Golden Hands Encyclopaedia of Embroidery, Collins, London, 1973

Gostelow, Mary, *Blackwork*, Batsford, London, 1976

Graeme-Robertson, E., *Sydney Lace, Ornamental Cast Iron*, Georgian House, Melbourne, Australia, 1962

'Guide to Textile Collections in Museums and Stately Homes', supplement to *Embroidery*, 33, 1982. Reprints available from the Embroiderers' Guild

Harding, Valerie, 'Blackwork and Spraying', *Embroidery*, 30, 1979, pp. 112–13

Howard, Constance, *Inspiration for Embroidery*, 2nd ed., Batsford, London, 1967

Kendrick, A. F., *Elizabethan Embroidery*, Batsford, London, 1933

Kendrick, A. F., *English Embroidery*, Batsford, London, 1913

Kiewe, H. E., 'Holbein's Influence on Elizabethan Embroidery', *Embroidery*, 7, 1956, pp. 73–6

Lemon, Jane, *Embroidered Boxes and Other Construction Techniques*, Faber & Faber, London, 1980; reprint, Batsford, 1984

McNeill, Moyra, 'Beginning Blackwork', *Embroidery*, 20, 1969, p. 119

McNeill, Moyra, 'Greetings in Blackwork', *Embroidery*, 28, 1977, pp. 48–9

Martin, Eileen, 'Blackwork', *Embroidery*, 28, 1977, pp. 84–5

Morris, May, 'Line Embroidery', *Art Worker's Quarterly*, no. 1, 1902, p. 117

Nevinson, J. L., *English Domestic Embroidery Catalogue*, Her Majesty's Stationery Office, London, 1950

Pascoe, Margaret, & Messent, Jan, *Blackwork*, ed. Kit Pyman, Needle Crafts 7, Search Press, London, 1979

Röttger, E., & Klante, D., *Creative Drawing: Point and Line*, Batsford, London, 1964

Sausmarez, de, Maurice, *Basic Design: The Dynamics of Visual Form*, Studio Vista/Van Nostrand Reinhold, New York, 1964

Thomas, Mary, *Mary Thomas's Embroidery Book*, Hodder & Stoughton, London, 1936

Tucker, Audrey, 'Design Development', *Embroidery*, 26, 1975, pp. 80–2

Wingfield-Digby, G. F., *Elizabethan Embroidery*, Faber & Faber, London, 1963

Where to See Historical Blackwork in the British Isles

Antony House
Torpoint
Cornwall
The Carew Pole Collection

The Museum of Costume
Bath
Avon

Royal Museum of Scotland
Edinburgh

Castle Gate Costume Museum
Nottingham
The Middleton Collection

Victoria and Albert Museum
South Kensington
London

Many other museums possess pieces of blackwork. It is always best to contact the curator before a proposed visit, as notice may be needed before a particular piece can be seen.

Index